The American Revolution in American History

This book is the eighth in a series in AEI's
"We Hold These Truths: America at 250" initiative.

WE HOLD THESE TRUTHS: AMERICA AT 250

Democracy and the American Revolution

Capitalism and the American Revolution

Religion and the American Revolution

Natural Rights, the Common Good, and the American Revolution

Slavery, Equality, and the American Revolution

The American Revolution and America's Role in the World

The American Revolution and the Constitution

The American Revolution in American History

The American Revolution in American History

Edited by Yuval Levin,
Adam J. White, and John Yoo

AEI Press
Publisher for the American Enterprise Institute
WASHINGTON, DC

ISBN-13: 978-0-8447-5115-3 (Paperback)

Library of Congress Cataloging in Publication data have been applied for.

Publisher for the American Enterprise Institute
for Public Policy Research
1789 Massachusetts Ave. NW
Washington, DC 20036
www.aei.org

Printed in the United States of America

Contents

Introduction

YUVAL LEVIN

July 4, 2026, will mark the 250th anniversary of the Declaration of Independence and, therefore, of the United States of America. In wondering how to properly observe and celebrate that event, Americans today are following in the footsteps of every generation since the American founding itself. The question of how we remember the American Revolution has always been a focal point for political debate and civic friction. But the celebration of our common inheritance also has always had the power to bring Americans together.

As we mark this seminal year, therefore, we can look to prior moments of patriotic celebration and reflection for guidance. The way the Revolution has been understood at different moments in our history is itself a crucial part of the Revolution's legacy. What the struggle for independence has meant to Americans in the past ought to be part of how we determine what it should mean to us now.

Key to what we learn when we consider the Revolution's place in the historical self-understandings of different generations of Americans is that the founding has always been used as a lens through which to view the present. In the lead-up to the Civil War, the Declaration of Independence was at the core of the debate over slavery, and Abraham Lincoln in particular made it his touchstone. Later in the 19th century, the Revolution came to be seen as the root of the risk-taking, venturesome spirit of both the Western frontier and the industrializing economy. In debates over the role of government in the first half of the 20th century, advocates of energetic centralized administration revived Alexander Hamilton's thought, while those who sought limits on federal power cited Thomas Jefferson instead. And during the Cold War, both capitalism and freedom were presented as direct extensions of the principles of the founding, while the movement for equal civil rights for black Americans emphasized the Declaration's commitment to the equality of all.

That pattern of appropriating the founding for contemporary political ends certainly continues in our time. Our debates about such divisive issues as executive power, social equality, immigration and national identity, and more call on the heroes and ideals of the American Revolution. Partisans of all sorts see the potential to advance their causes in a year when Americans' attention is once again directed to our nation's origins.

But even as these arguments of the moment look to the moral vocabulary of the Revolution for support, some of the founding's fundamental tenets continue to insist on their own distinct and timeless relevance. This, too, has long been evident to Americans with a historical perspective. As the nation celebrated the 150th anniversary of the founding in 1926, President Calvin Coolidge took note of that timelessness in remarks at Independence Hall in Philadelphia:

> It is often asserted that the world has made a great deal of progress since 1776, that we have had new thoughts and new experiences which have given us a great advance over the people of that day, and that we may therefore very well discard their conclusions for something more modern. But that reasoning can not be applied to this great charter. If all men are created equal, that is final. If they are endowed with inalienable rights, that is final. If governments derive their just powers from the consent of the governed, that is final. No advance, no progress can be made beyond these propositions. If anyone wishes to deny their truth or their soundness, the only direction in which he can proceed historically is not forward, but backward toward the time when there was no equality, no rights of the individual, no rule of the people. Those who wish to proceed in that direction can not lay claim to progress. They

> are reactionary. Their ideas are not more modern, but more ancient, than those of the Revolutionary fathers.[1]

The finality that defines the Declaration's fundamental arguments is why they stand as durable standards for American life and why Americans in very different times and circumstances have appealed to them. Understanding the Declaration and the memory of the Revolution is therefore essential to better understanding America.

Better understanding America is precisely the purpose of the American Enterprise Institute's "We Hold These Truths: America at 250" initiative, an ambitious celebration of the founding of which this volume forms a part. Over several years leading up to the anniversary of the Declaration of Independence, we have invited scholars both within AEI and from other institutions to take up a series of themes important to understanding the American Revolution. These scholars represent a variety of fields and viewpoints, so they approach each of these themes from various angles. The papers they have produced have been published in a series of edited volumes intended to help Americans think more deeply and clearly about our nation's origins, character, and prospects.

The American Revolution in American History is the eighth and final of those books. Its chapters began as papers presented at an AEI conference held at Thomas Jefferson's Monticello on September 3, 2025. Other volumes in the series consider the American Revolution in relation to other themes, such as democracy, religion, natural rights, and global affairs. In each case, our goal is to help reintroduce readers to their nation's history, thereby enabling them to maturely appreciate the reasons for celebrating the extraordinary milestone of its 250th anniversary.

In the chapters that follow, five eminent scholars of history and government consider the ways in which the American Revolution has been interpreted in different periods of our history.

Richard Brookhiser traces how the story of the founding has been told in popular culture—particularly in works of popular history, drama, and art—and finds a great deal to appreciate.

Jane Kamensky examines the depiction of the American Revolution in film and considers why the high drama of the War of Independence has never been properly translated into a good movie.

Allen C. Guelzo looks at how Americans in the first hundred years of our national life used and misused the Revolution and what lessons we who are much further from those great events might draw from earlier interpreters.

Rita Koganzon assesses the changing ways in which American textbooks have taught the Revolution over the past 250 years, finding that the legacy of 1776 has been presented to students variously as sets of exemplars to emulate, systems to manage, and structures to resist.

Wilfred McClay argues that Americans have always fought about the meaning of the American Revolution but for that very reason have always also found in it much inspiration for a shared love of country.

All of these arguments suggest that history can never fully stand apart from its subjects. That is surely true of the very project of which this volume forms the final installment. We have sought not just to shine a light on the people, events, and ideas that defined the founding era but to invite readers to reflect on what their struggles and achievements illuminate about our own time—and the American future we all will build in common.

Notes

1. Calvin Coolidge, "Address at the Celebration of the 150th Anniversary of the Declaration of Independence in Philadelphia, Pennsylvania," July 5, 1926, American Presidency Project, https://www.presidency.ucsb.edu/node/267359.

1

The American Revolution Today

RICHARD BROOKHISER

Only oblivion ends wars. As long they are remembered, the issues are still in play; the shots, rhetorical and sometimes actual, are still being fired. All the more so with wars that are revolutionary as well as military or merely political.

So, how is the American Revolution going these days? There are no remaining partisans of the British (outside Canada) and few who think the Revolution was insignificant. One of the latter, and that for the space of only one tale, was Washington Irving. The 20-year sleep of Rip Van Winkle in Irving's story of the same name spans the Revolution. Before his encounter in the Catskill Mountains with Henry Hudson's crew and their mysterious drink, Rip spends his days lounging at the village inn, which bears an image of George III on its signboard. When Rip wakes, he finds, among all the other changes that confront him, that the inn has been torn down and replaced by a hotel. The signboard still hangs, but with a cocked hat painted over the crown; the George it celebrates is Washington.

Rip walks into the middle of a campaign rally, with a speaker "haranguing vehemently about rights of citizens—election—members of congress—liberty—Bunker's Hill—heroes of seventy-six—and other words, that were a perfect Babylonish jargon" to him. When he finally understands what has happened, he passively accepts the new order of things, for he is "no politician; the changes of states and empires [make] but little impression on him." All he cares about is that the wife who once nagged him has passed away. The American Revolution—no big deal.[1]

This was not Irving's settled view. He was named for George Washington, and his last literary work, valiantly finished in a struggle against illness, was a biography of his namesake. Most Americans in his lifetime and since have agreed with him and not with Rip that the Revolution was indeed a big deal. Their disagreements are over what it meant.

The Revolution has long had critics, no longer Tories but leftists. Early in the 20th century, progressive historians of Charles A. Beard's school depicted it as a power play of colonial elites whose rhetoric invoked liberty but whose intentions were to run affairs for their own benefit. Late in the century, Howard Zinn, communist turned new leftist, made essentially the same argument about the Revolution (and every other era of America history) in *A People's History of the United States* and spin-off books, which continue to be widely read and taught even after his death, in 2010. Yet there are reasons to think the Revolution is well remembered. It is taken seriously and, within the requirements of the forms that tell its story, depicted accurately.

Popular History

For years, the Revolution and the period of which it was the fulcrum, called for convenience's sake "the founding," occupied a special place in the academy. Waves of theory, nakedly political or ornately whimsical, buffeted the humanities in the last decades of the 20th century. (What happened to my undergraduate major, English, was memorialized in the satires of David Lodge.) Yet the teaching of American history, 1763 to 1800, mostly escaped. Douglass Adair's World War II–era dissertation, *The Intellectual Origins of Jeffersonian Democracy*, had set the tone. Adair and scholarly peers like Bernard Bailyn and Edmund Morgan began their efforts to understand what the people they were studying did by trying to understand what they thought they were doing. They addressed the Americans in question not as conscripts in the class war but as agents with ideas that had consequences.

Bailyn began one of his works, *The Origins of American Politics*, with a swipe at a young Woodrow Wilson, who complained as a graduate student about having to learn "one or two hundred dates and one or two thousand minute particulars about the quarrels of nobody knows who with an obscure [colonial] Governor, for nobody knows what. Just think of all that energy wasted!" Not wasted, said Bailyn. Those quarrels produced the American Revolution and American politics.[2]

There were scholarly disputes about what those ideas were and how they worked out in the world. Were founding-era Americans old Romans? English country party polemicists? Magi come to herald the birth of Abraham Lincoln (which is roughly the view of the West Coast Straussians)? Whatever the ideas of the time were and wherever they came from, there was a built-in background consensus among historians that the American mix that resulted was both novel and consequential. That is what the historians' subjects themselves believed. Late 18th-century Americans and late 20th-century scholars were on the same page.

Old scholars died or retired. One of the latter, on the faculty of a high-end Northeastern college, told me that when he stepped down he expected to be replaced not by another scholar of the public life of his period but by a specialist in looms. What he meant was that the tools of production and the culture, material and social, of spinners and other humble folk would take precedence over the ideas, arguments, and slogans of elites and humble folk alike. This, we agreed, would be a loss. There is a lot to be learned from looms, but they are not *The American Crisis*.

The career of Joanne Freeman, who belongs to a younger generation of historians, is an interesting case study. She loves Alexander Hamilton and edited the Library of America's volume of his writings. But in the academy when she was coming up you couldn't write just another book about Hamilton. So her first book (and first hit), *Affairs of Honor*, was about the duel that took his life—and the early republic's culture of political challenge and response in which dueling was embedded. *The Field of Blood* carried her studies up to the Civil War, focusing on violent encounters in Congress, where the caning of abolitionist Senator Charles Sumner by an enraged proslavery congressman was only one of many incidents and not the most destructive. Fascinating stuff.

But dead Hamilton and bleeding Sumner might ask, "Is that what we were about?"

Just as the political and intellectual paradigm of the Revolution began to fade in the academy, it began to colonize the bestseller lists. A wave of books by serious popular authors (including David McCullough and Ron Chernow) and academics who could write (such as Morgan and Joseph Ellis) racked up sales and literary prizes in the early 2000s. Most of these historical bestsellers were biographies: McCullough resurrected John Adams; Chernow, Hamilton. Morgan wrote about Benjamin Franklin, Ellis about everybody. The form of a life story—subject is born, does things, dies—was readily comprehensible, and the incidents of a well-told life could provide the drama, beyond even politics and warfare, that Freeman had found on the dueling ground.

The popularity of such books reflected the public's desire for ongoing postgraduate education. Amazon and Barnes & Noble could be what college history departments had once been and were beginning no longer to be. Inheriting the role of the academic studies that had been their forebears, they shared the same view of the late 18th-century American world: Something important had happened then that still speaks, or should speak, to us now.

There were critics along the way. In 2003, H. W. Brands wrote an essay in *The Atlantic* titled "Founders Chic." "Our reverence for the Fathers," declared the subhead, "has gotten out of hand."[3] But Brands himself had contributed to the founding hit parade three years earlier with *The First American*, a biography of Franklin. He would return to the scene of the crime in the 2020s with books on Patriot-versus-Loyalist strife in the Revolution and the quarrels of Thomas Jefferson, Hamilton, and James Madison that birthed the first American two-party system. We pay too much attention to the period, it seems, and we can't not.

Before Americans become college students or elders looking to fill in their educations, they go to grade school and high school. Here one must note the activities of the Gilder Lehrman Institute of American History. Richard Gilder (1932–2020) and Lewis Lehrman (1938–2026) were philanthropists with a lifelong passion for the subject. They amassed an archive of 87,000 documents, made available as primary sources to students and teachers via publications, seminars in person and online, and traveling exhibitions. The archive's main subject is slavery and the Civil War. (Gilder and Lehrman also cofounded the Gilder Lehrman Center for the Study of Slavery, Resistance, and Abolition at Yale.) Close in second is the founding period.

Now, the institute serves a network of 36,000 affiliated schools. A perennial gee-whiz anecdote of American self-flagellation is how many kids today don't know hugely important names or dates, like what century World War II happened in. If they don't know when the American Revolution happened, it is not the fault of the Gilder Lehrman Institute.[4]

History as Drama

The work that historians produce and students consume, whether in school or later, consists overwhelmingly of words. But words on paper, or on the screens of our devices, are not the only way the past is remembered, or even the most potent. Two media that have presented the American Revolution intelligently are musical theater and painting. There is ample precedent for doing so. Although the American musical is a newish form, scarcely a century old, that rarely addresses history directly, history plays have been produced for a long time, back through Shakespeare to Aeschylus. Paintings and other visual art forms—mosaics, friezes, sculptures—have depicted rulers, generals, and their battles for as many centuries.

Contestants for the Tony Award for Best Musical in 1969 included two shows by old Broadway hands (*Zorba*, with songs by John Kander and Fred Ebb, and *Promises, Promises*, with a book by Neil Simon and songs by Burt Bacharach and Hal David) and one sprung from the zeitgeist (Gerôme Ragni and James Rado's *Hair*). The show that beat them all was *1776*, with songs by Sherman Edwards and a book by Peter Stone.

The victory was in many ways remarkable. The show is talk heavy, more like a play with musical numbers. Taking place in a few rooms in Philadelphia, *1776* is a drama about the politics of an action: declaring independence after 15 months of warfare. Who backed it, who needed convincing, how the deed was done—these questions supply the drama.

The most vivid characters are three of the most important, all portrayed as they actually were: John Adams as vain, combative, and ardent; Benjamin Franklin as jokey when he had to be, savvy always; and George Washington as speaking only through dispatches from the battlefield, a model of desperate resolution. Thomas Jefferson is a bit of a cipher, a vacancy justified by his real-life shyness. In one production I saw, his best moment came as he listened, in an anteroom, to the first reading of his immortal document and glanced at a lion and unicorn fixed to the wall: symbols of Britain's imperium, to be banished forever from the newborn states.

There are mischaracterizations of lesser figures. Continental congressmen John Dickinson and James Wilson, who reflected the reluctance of Pennsylvania's Quaker and merchant classes to cut ties with Britain, appear as cartoon villains—Dickinson sinister, Wilson bumbling and timid. Neither of them was either of those things. Richard Henry Lee of Virginia comes across as a well-dressed yokel, a genial boob, when he was in fact an austere and striking orator who emphasized his points with gestures of his right hand, maimed in a hunting accident and wrapped in black silk.

There are also only two parts for women, only one of them good. Martha Jefferson, brought in to inspire her husband to buckle down and write the Declaration, seems obviously tacked on. The only real passion onstage exists between John and Abigail Adams. Since they were hundreds of miles apart in the summer of 1776—he in Philadelphia, she at home in Braintree, Massachusetts—they show it only in sung correspondence.

1776's most dramatic song is sung by one of the delegates who most needs convincing. Edward Rutledge of South Carolina demands that a passage in Jefferson's draft blaming Britain for foisting slavery on its colonies be cut. When delegates from Northern states defend the passage, Rutledge strides to the footlights and sings "Molasses to Rum," a dark paean to the slave trade and the Northern shippers who batten on it, complete with auctioneer's patter. We Carolinians own them, but you Yankees bring them to us.

To win the Deep South's support for independence, the offending passage goes. What is the audience meant to think of that deal? The musical gives us two options. Franklin, the pragmatist, calls it a necessary bargain in pursuit of independence. "We're men—no more, no less—trying to get a nation started against greater odds than a more generous God would have allowed."[5] Adams, the idealist, foresees an independence finally leading to liberty for all. "I see Americans, *all* Americans, / Free! For evermore!"[6] Theatergoers know that Adams was right, though it would take a civil war and a civil rights movement to make him so.

For all its depiction of all-too-human politics and compromising compromises, *1776* ends with a triumphant tableau of delegates affixing their signatures in ratification of what they, and we, believe was a deed well done. *1776* was made into a film in 1972 and revived on Broadway in 1997 and 2022. There is every reason to think that, despite its large cast—always an economic drawback for potential producers—*1776* will march on, although it must now share space with a second revolutionary show.

Lin-Manuel Miranda, who had written the award-winning musical *In the Heights*, turned his thoughts to Hamilton after reading Chernow's biography on a vacation. He began with a mixtape of songs, one of which he sang at a White House poetry night in 2009. The video of the performance is online;[7] the Obamas and other members of the audience seem pleased, if mildly surprised. *Hamilton: An American Musical* premiered off-Broadway in January 2015, moving to Broadway that summer, and since it has conquered the world. The show won 11 Tonys, and the cast album topped the *Billboard* rap album chart for 10 weeks.

The show follows the arc of Hamilton's life, coming from nowhere, rising to the top of his adopted new nation, and dying at the hands of his frenemy Aaron Burr. Hamilton's love for his wife, Eliza Schuyler Hamilton, and his bewitchment by the con woman Maria Reynolds supply personal drama and women's parts. (Two of Eliza's sisters also appear.) But the focus of the show, as in *1776*, is on the public story.

This occurs in two halves. Act 1 depicts the American Revolution. The antagonist is George III; in an amusing cameo, he sings to America in the voice of a rejected, abusive lover. The inspiration is Washington, on whose staff Hamilton serves. As in *1776*, Washington is shown as the resolute commander in chief, but now he is also an anchor of seriousness for Hamilton and the nation. "Dying is easy, young man," he instructs his protégé at one point, "Living is harder."[8] Struggle is noble, and victory is the reward, but after victory comes more struggle.

Act 2 takes the story forward into the postwar beginnings of the early republic, and it is, surprisingly, a Federalist Party campaign tract. The antagonists here are Jefferson and Madison, presented as a fop and a conniving gnome, respectively. Washington and Hamilton want to build a prosperous, stable nation; Jefferson and Madison want their own advancement. In both halves of the show Burr is a somewhat puzzled spectator, wishing he had Hamilton's access to power and greatness and almost sorry he has to shoot him.

Miranda used a variety of musical styles—George III sings like a creepy Paul McCartney—but his default choice was rap, whose high word counts allowed him to convey a blizzard of information. There are the inevitable speedups and shortcuts—the Marquis de Lafayette appears as Hamilton's chum years before he actually arrived in America; Jefferson and Madison confront Hamilton personally with evidence of his love affair, when the confronting was in fact done by their ally James Monroe. Yet the general level of accuracy is high, the level of detail amazingly so. A musical about the American Revolution that manages to depict the New York Loyalist Samuel Seabury is digging deep indeed.

Miranda's innovation was to cast non-white actors in almost all the roles. (He played Hamilton in the show's original run.) This was more than a nontraditional casting stunt: It made the point that America—Hamilton's

America—was what Adams had foreseen in 1776, a new country in which all would be free forevermore. Yet there is a peculiar twist.

Miranda's identification with Hamilton rests on their shared connection with the Caribbean. As Hamilton—born on Nevis, raised on Saint Croix—came from the islands; so had Miranda's father, born and raised in Puerto Rico. Taking his cue from his own family history, Miranda presented the aspiring new America as one of immigrants rather than people of color. "Immigrants: We get the job done," declares a song from Act 1.[9] Slavery plays a curiously small part in the show's drama. "Molasses to Rum" is far blunter about the institution than anything Miranda composed.

The Federalist partisanship of Act 2 follows an old dynamic of historical remembrance. Neither Jefferson nor Hamilton has ever quite left the pantheon, but their reputations, like objects hanging from the rod of a mobile, have risen and fallen in opposition since their lifetimes. Jefferson had a good half century beginning in the 1930s when Franklin Roosevelt put his face on the nickel and his monument alongside the Tidal Basin in Washington, DC. Jefferson's Declaration could be invoked against the rising tide of fascism, and his polemics against Hamilton's economic program could seem prophetic of Roosevelt's against Wall Street.

At century's end, increased attention to slavery and Jefferson's liaison with his slave Sally Hemings caused Jefferson to dip and Hamilton, who helped found the New-York Manumission Society, to rise. Did that mean that Hamiltonian economics, so favorable to investors (or speculators), rose too? Critics on the left grumbled at the prospect, and Miranda came in for flak as a neoliberal naïf. Envy was also at work. Miranda's detractors have yet to make it to Broadway.

For years, *Hamilton* was inescapable. *The New York Times*' offices in Manhattan, ran the joke, had an entire floor devoted to writers churning out stories about it. The son of a friend of mine, 12 years old, claimed to be able to answer any question put to him with an apposite line from the show's book.

That rapture is over. The *Times* and my friend's son moved on to new obsessions: the *Times* to the 1619 Project, the boy to zombies. But the

Source: Emanuel Leutze, *Washington Crossing the Delaware*, 1851, oil on canvas, 149 × 255 in., Metropolitan Museum of Art, New York, https://www.metmuseum.org/art/collection/search/11417.

show is still running on Broadway and in touring productions. The Gilder Lehrman Institute produced a study guide to accompany a student-ticket program. Once again, America has a musical that is a heartfelt celebration of a great hope, greatly realized.

History as Imagery

Musicals depend on performance. They exist only when they are revived, or at least when one's device plays a recording. Paintings exist as long as their canvases and pigments last, silently awaiting new viewers. Two paintings depicting episodes from the American Revolution have imprinted themselves on America's mind's eye.

Emanuel Leutze, born in 1816 in Württemberg, immigrated with his parents to Philadelphia, where he first studied painting. Over the course of his life, he moved back and forth between America and Europe. In 1850, to encourage European liberals thrilled by the revolutions of 1848, then disappointed by their failure, he painted a scene from the American Revolution: *Washington Crossing the Delaware.*

The Trenton-Princeton campaign in the winter of 1776 marked a turning point in the struggle for independence. After six months of disasters, in which Washington was driven from New York City and across New Jersey into Pennsylvania, he managed to return over the Delaware River and hand his pursuers two small but stinging defeats, which ended Britain's hopes of wrapping up the war quickly. With his signature literary flourish, Mason Locke Weems, Washington's first biographer, made the army's nighttime passage of the river the perilous symbol of the entire operation:

> Washington and his little forlorn hope, pressed on through the darksome night, pelted by an incessant storm of hail and snow. On approaching the river, nine miles above Trenton, they heard the unwelcome roar of ice, loud crashing along the angry flood. . . . The troops were instantly embarked, and after

> five hours of infinite toil and danger, landed, some of them frost-bitten.[10]

Leutze painted two large copies of the scene. The first would be destroyed in an air raid on Bremen in World War II; the second was shipped to New York in 1851, where 50,000 people saw it, including an eight-year-old Henry James. "We gaped responsive to every item," he remembered, "lost in the marvel of the wintry light, of the sharpness of the ice-blocks."[11]

Leutze created a hyperreal image of a little American armada, crossing the Delaware from right to left. The canvas is dominated by the lead boat, in which Washington stands, gazing literally at New Jersey, symbolically at the future. The American flag next to him is borne by 18-year-old Lieutenant James Monroe. The clothing of the figures in the boat shows that they are Americans of different regions and classes: Virginia gentlemen, Philadelphia merchants, New England sailors, frontier riflemen. As David Hackett Fischer explained in his book *Washington's Crossing*, they are all in the same boat.

The long hair of the red-jacketed oarsman on the port side has led some to suppose that he is in fact a she. During the Revolutionary War, a handful of women slipped into the ranks dressed as men. Women of the army served officially as nurses and cooks and sometimes fought, the most famous being Mary Ludwig Hays, better known as Molly Pitcher, who swabbed her husband's cannon at the Battle of Monmouth.

The identification of a woman here is probably fanciful. Not fanciful is the black oarsman near the starboard bow. The regiment that manned the boats on the night of the crossing was the 14th Massachusetts, composed of sailors from Marblehead, including blacks and Native Americans. (Readers of *Moby-Dick* will know about the diversity of ships' crews.) The 14th Massachusetts were not immigrants, but they got the job done.[12]

Washington Crossing the Delaware ended up in the collection of the Metropolitan Museum of Art in New York. It is a huge canvas, about

21 feet by 12 feet. In the 21st century it was given an elaborate carved gilt frame, matching the one it had when first shown. Since the painting is too large to be carried out the door of the room in which it hangs, the work of reframing had to be done on the spot. The painting regularly makes lists of the most famous and must-see works in the Met's collections.[13]

John Trumbull, born in 1756, was a veteran of the American Revolution who served briefly on the staffs of Washington and Horatio Gates. His father, Jonathan Trumbull Sr., was governor of Connecticut, which allowed John to meet everyone who counted. He went to London to study painting with the American-born Benjamin West and absorbed the innovations in history painting that West and another American émigré, John Singleton Copley, were making. Sir Joshua Reynolds, the greatest British painter of the day, thought figures in contemporary history paintings should be portrayed in classical, or at least timeless, garments so as not to distract from their actions and characters. West and Copley went the other way, loading their canvases with details of weapons, uniforms, and other accoutrements.

Trumbull envisioned an innovation of his own: He would not confine himself to portraits of great contemporaries or scenes of single events but would execute a series of paintings that told the history of the American Revolution. It took him over 45 years of a long and often distracted life, but by 1832 he finished eight paintings, which he donated to Yale College.

Trumbull was proud of his military career. In a midlife self-portrait he showed himself sitting near his palette but holding his sword, as though his service was more important to him than his talent was. His series is tilted toward the military: Three paintings show battles (Bunker Hill, Quebec, and Princeton) and three surrenders (Trenton, Saratoga, and Yorktown), while one, *General George Washington Resigning His Commission*, shows a scene in Congress, half populated by men in uniform (Washington, come to give his commission up, and the comrades who have accompanied him).

One painting is entirely civilian: *Declaration of Independence*. This is the painter's vision of what Stone and Edwards put onstage. Trumbull got the

Source: John Trumbull, *General George Washington Resigning His Commission*, 1824, oil on canvas, 12 × 18 ft., Capitol Rotunda, Washington, DC, https://www.aoc.gov/explore-capitol-campus/art/general-george-washington-resigning-his-commission.

idea from Jefferson himself, when Jefferson was minister to France in the late 1780s and Trumbull, studying art in Paris, was his houseguest. Jefferson made a drawing of the floor plan of the room in which the Continental Congress had met; on the bottom of the paper, Trumbull made his first sketch of the scene.

Trumbull shows the five members of the drafting committee—Adams, Roger Sherman, Robert Livingston, Jefferson, and Franklin—presenting their handiwork to John Hancock, the president of the Continental Congress. Behind and around them the other delegates to Congress spread out, sitting or standing. Jefferson is the tallest man in the room and the brightest—Trumbull has put him in a red waistcoat. Adams stands in the dead center of the composition. Franklin is the only man in it looking directly at us. A few of the delegates are talking among themselves, but the great majority and we, the viewers, are paying attention to what the drafting committee is offering.

We cannot see any of Jefferson's words on the piece of paper that Hancock is receiving, yet the painting, mute though it is, tells us important things about the nation the delegates were expecting to make. There is a war going on, as captured enemy flags and drums hanging as trophies on the back wall of the room remind us. But every man here is in ordinary civilian dress. This is not a revolution of generals, as Haiti's and Latin America's will be or France's will become.

The clothing also shows us that these men are broadly similar. A few are enormously wealthy—when Charles Carroll of Maryland signed, someone purportedly cracked, "There go a few millions"—others merely prosperous.[14] None are noble; there are no coronets, ermines, or chains of rank. Aristocratic orders have gone by the wayside.

These men, finally, have deliberated; they are behaving deliberately now. There are no impassioned salutes. Trumbull saw the stiff-armed Romans of Jacques-Louis David's 1784 *Oath of the Horatii* in David's studio in Paris; their gestures would be repeated in David's sketch of *Tennis Court Oath* at the dawn of the French Revolution. But America's revolutionaries swore too: The Declaration's signers pledged lives, fortunes, and sacred

Source: John Trumbull, *Declaration of Independence*, 1818, oil on canvas, 12 × 18 ft., Capitol Rotunda, Washington, DC, https://www.aoc.gov/explore-capitol-campus/art/declaration-independence.

honor. Four would be captured during the war, and one would have to hide in a cave; thousands of the soldiers they sent into combat would die. But as they fought—as the fighting went on—they thought, discussed, and decided.

Trumbull painted his *Declaration* in 1787. The original three-foot-by-two-foot canvas hangs at Yale. A larger, half-life-sized copy hangs with four other enlarged paintings from his revolutionary series at the Wadsworth Atheneum Museum of Art in Hartford. But the one that millions of people see is the life-sized copy displayed with three of its fellows (*Surrender of General Burgoyne*, *Surrender of Lord Cornwallis*, and *General George Washington Resigning His Commission*) in the Capitol Rotunda in Washington, DC.

Trumbull's *Declaration* is reproduced in textbooks, in history books, and on the reverse of the two-dollar bill. It is the necessary pendant to Trumbull's and Leutze's and everyone else's battle scenes. It shows what the Revolution was fought for. Ideas sometimes have to be secured by combat before they can become real in the world—a lesson for thinkers. Wars have to be guided by ideas or they become scrambles for dominance—a lesson for warriors.

Not all who see the *Declaration* or Trumbull's other paintings understand them. On January 6, 2021, one of the protesters who invaded the Capitol was photographed toting the Speaker of the House's lectern across the Rotunda with *Surrender of General Burgoyne* in the background. There were riots and worse before and during the Revolution; they are the static of all revolutions, when they are not the main current. But they were not what Trumbull painted or what his subjects led or expected to use in governing. Most viewers will get the message; Trumbull made it as plain as he could.

Source: John Trumbull, *Surrender of General Burgoyne*, 1821, oil on canvas, 12 × 18 ft., Capitol Rotunda, Washington, DC, https://www.aoc.gov/explore-capitol-campus/art/surrender-general-burgoyne.

The Revolution Lives On

A shelf of books, two musicals, two paintings—that is not a bad account of the American Revolution to start. It grabs the attention; on further reading, listening, or viewing, it reveals deeper meanings.

A lot in our lives competes with even great events of the past, let alone all the other events past, current, and to come: work, fun and games, and the backward pull of time. But we still live with the country and the institutions the revolutionaries made. It is worth a little trouble understanding them. Many Americans through the years have taken that trouble, and many still do.

Notes

1. Washington Irving, "Rip Van Winkle: A Posthumous Writing of Dietrich Knickerbocker.," in *The Sketch Book of Geoffrey Crayon, Gent.* (New York, 1819), 1:83, 92.

2. Bernard Bailyn, *The Origins of American Politics* (Alfred A. Knopf, 1968), 8–9.

3. H. W. Brands, "Founders Chic," *The Atlantic*, September 2003, https://www.theatlantic.com/magazine/archive/2003/09/founders-chic/302773/.

4. Gilder Lehrman Institute of American History, "About," www.gilderlehrman.org/about.

5. *1776: A Musical Play*, book by Peter Stone (Viking, 1970), 132.

6. "Is Anybody There?," music and lyrics by Sherman Edwards, in *1776*, 128.

7. Obama White House, "Lin-Manuel Miranda Performs at the White House Poetry Jam: (8 of 8)," YouTube, November 2, 2009, https://www.youtube.com/watch?v=WNFf7nMIGnE.

8. "Right Hand Man," music and lyrics by Lin-Manuel Miranda, in *Hamilton: The Revolution*, by Lin-Manuel Miranda and Jeremy McCarter (Grand Central, 2016), 64.

9. "Yorktown (The World Turned Upside Down)," music and lyrics by Lin-Manuel Miranda, in Miranda and McCarter, *Hamilton*, 121.

10. Mason L. Weems, *A History of the Life and Death, Virtues and Exploits of General George Washington* [. . .] (1800; J. B. Lippincott, 1918), 111.

11. *Henry James: Autobiography*, ed. Frederick W. Dupee (Criterion Books, 1956), 152.

12. David Hackett Fischer, *Washington's Crossing* (Oxford University Press, 2004), 22.

13. Carrie Rebora Barratt et al., "*Washington Crossing the Delaware*": *Restoring an American Masterpiece* (Metropolitan Museum of Art, 2011), 43–45.

14. Edward Currier, *The Political Text Book* [. . .] (Holliston, MA, 1841), 22. The quotation appears without attribution, so it is not clear whether the line was really uttered.

2

The American Revolution at the Movies

JANE KAMENSKY

For as long as cinema has existed, people have made movies about the American Revolution. Thomas Edison shot *Bowling Green* around 1896, a date often used to mark the beginnings of the art form.[1] Movies exploring the nation's founding have kept coming in fits and starts ever since, spanning genres from drama to western, fantasy, comedy, musical, and yes, pornography. (Not to be overlooked: *The Spirit of Seventy Sex* appears to have been the only theatrical release sort of about the founding to debut in the nation's bicentennial year.) The filmed version of *Hamilton: An American Musical*, for which Disney paid a whopping $75 million in 2020, is the most recent major entry in the canon.[2] Surely it will not be the last.

And yet, throughout that century and a quarter, movies about the beginnings of the United States have been, almost without exception, stinkers. The problem isn't chiefly one of material or talent. *The Spy* (1914), one of the first major studio releases on the subject, was, after all, "Written by the Greatest Writer of Indian Stories, James Fenimore Cooper. Produced by the Great Special Feature Director, Otis Turner," and "Acted by an Exceptional Cast," as *Billboard* crowed.[3] And still, pffft.

Generations of decorated playwrights, novelists, historians, lyricists, and dramaturges; top-grossing directors; bankable stars—all have foundered on the shoals of the Revolution. None has produced a standard-setting work of film or history, let alone both. There is no American Revolution battle picture with the punch-in-the-gut impact of *Glory* (1989), *Saving Private Ryan* (1998), or *Platoon* (1986). No biopic with the insight of *Lincoln* (2012) or *Patton* (1970) or, lest you mutter, "It can't be done for ye olden days," *Amadeus* (1984). Despite the prolonged impact of the long war for independence on those left behind and a profusion of excellent recent scholarship on women who traveled with the armies, there is no home-front drama with the resonance of *The Best Years of Our Lives* (1946) or *The Deer Hunter* (1978). And no cinematic breakthrough like *The Birth of a Nation* (1915). If D. W. Griffith's Redemptionist spectacle wrote history with lightning, as Woodrow Wilson is alleged to have said, his Revolution picture, *America* (1924), wrote it with a soggy breadstick.[4]

Why has so much money and talent chased a story so dramatic and important for so many years with so little to show for the hunt? "It remains one of the mysteries of the American cinema why the incredibly dramatic and complex birth of the nation has provided such infertile ground for motion pictures," *Variety* opined in 2000, before making the boneheaded claim that Roland Emmerich's *The Patriot*, starring Mel Gibson, had cracked the case.[5] *The Patriot*, a.k.a. *Braveheart Part Deux*, did no such thing. Still, the question is a good one. For the failures, in all their box-office-bombing glory, have something to tell us about not only the shifting shapes of American culture but also the Revolution itself.

But what? In pursuit of answers, not to mention happiness, I screened a spate of American Revolution pictures with the least randomized, most unrepresentative of focus groups: a couple dozen members of Monticello's staff. We are deeply and perhaps to a distorting degree committed to holding "these truths," though we tried not to let our penchant for historical fact get in the way of a good story when there was one to be found, which was pretty much never. We ate a lot of popcorn, endured a gaggle of turkeys, and hypothesized some truths about why depictions of the Revolution on the silver screen struggle with beginnings, endings, scope, and scale that are less than "self-evident" but may help our own storytelling for 2026 and beyond.

The Problem of Beginnings

If you've ever graded a student's paper on any subject, you know something of the problem of beginnings: that tendency to circle the airport at 30,000 feet, describing the clouds, before finally touching down three paragraphs later. The problem of beginnings is a transcendent narrative challenge, faced by every creator in every medium. The American Revolution offers a particular case in point, for it is an origin story, and as in many origin stories, there is always a turtle beneath the turtle on whose back the world rests. It's hard for a director to begin a story about the first turtle when it's turtles all the way down.

Before I blame John Ford—and blame him I must—let me acknowledge that people of the founding generation recognized the challenge. In 1818, John Adams wrote to the Baltimore newspaper editor Hezekiah Niles, asking, "What do We mean by the American Revolution?" The transformation had been longer and deeper than the war itself. "The Revolution was in the Minds and Hearts of the People. A Change in their Religious Sentiments of their Duties and Obligations," he suggested. *That* shift—"the real American Revolution"—Adams dated to "the Annihilation of the French Dominion in America," around about 1760. Others pushed what Adams called "an awakening and a revival of American Principles and Feelings" still earlier.[6] Thomas Jefferson argued in 1774 that something in the character of the remote Saxon ancestry of British émigrés to North America had predisposed them to free trade, rights claiming, and perhaps even independence.[7]

A great deal of scholarship about the Revolution has followed suit, paring the onion, layer by layer, to find the points of national origin. Starting the road to the American Revolution at the forks of the Monongahela in 1754 may be a perfectly reasonable strategy for a college textbook. But it's a disaster for a feature film hoping to accomplish its business in something under three hours.[8] There are good reasons Oliver Stone didn't begin *Platoon* with the French colonization of Indochina, nor Steven Spielberg *Schindler's List* (1993) with the expulsion of Jews from Spain in 1492.

Movie after movie, for decade after decade, has failed to convincingly establish the beginning of the revolutionary plot, attempting instead to tell the whole story of the whole of *us*. Griffith's silent *America* opens at some nondescript moment in the 1760s with establishing shots of families playing innocently as soldiers on Lexington Green. Title cards allude to George III and his "evil counselors," as well as to the deposed Massachusetts Governor Francis Bernard, no more a household name in 1924 than he is a century later.[9]

The fighting started before the opening frames of Ford's *Drums Along the Mohawk*, his founding-as-Western epic. Released in 1939, the same year as *Gone with the Wind* and *The Wizard of Oz*, the visual markers of *Drums Along the Mohawk* are so generically "ye olden days" that the production might conceivably have reused costumes from either of those—and possibly both. Log forts, covered wagons, hoopskirts, and indeterminate Injuns seem to have wandered in from other Ford films set in the transmountain West. Visually, as my sons might say, it's giving *1849*.[10]

The Howards of Virginia, a black-and-white 1940 Cary Grant vehicle that numbers among the best of this motley lot, begins in 1754 with its protagonists as schoolchildren and has to grow an entire adult cast before Patrick Henry can thunder his clarion call for liberty or death at the Virginia Convention in Richmond.[11]

In a couple of the zaniest films that could conceivably fit under the big battle tent of the Revolutionary War picture, the squishiness of time is signal rather than noise. Abbott and Costello's raucous ghost story, *The Time of Their Lives*, released in 1946 as a seemingly conscious send-up of *The Best Years of Our Lives*, tacks between the Benedict Arnold and Major John André conspiracy of 1780 and its present day, with plenty of in-jokes about the moviemaking itself. ("Pardon me, didn't I see you in *Rebecca*?" asks a visitor to Danbury Manor of the creepy Mrs. Danvers–style housekeeper.) As the modern-day players search for a letter from George Washington that's the key to the slapstick mystery, another muses, "From butler to psychiatrist in six generations—now that's democracy for you!"[12]

A gentler and wiser then-and-now humor animates *Sweet Liberty* (1986), written by, directed by, and starring Alan Alda, about whom I will not say an unkind word because he reminds me of my dad.[13] Alda plays Michael Burgess, a motorcycle-riding professor of history at a fictional college who has written a deeply researched book about the very real 1781 Battle of Cowpens that's being turned into a film. Michael Caine plays the dual role of actor Elliott James and character Banastre Tarleton as delicious dastards—duelists and winking lechers. The plot gets its energy from the filming of a movie within the movie, as the Hollywood adaptation of Burgess's book pits the professor's faithfulness to the past against the hungers of the box office.

"So I changed a couple of the jokes!" says the scriptwriter, played by Bob Hoskins.

"It didn't have any jokes!" Burgess thunders back. "The American Revolution was not a goddamned vaudeville show!"[14] Alda's character spends much of the film in piqued astonishment about how little people know and how much less they care about the period to which he's devoted his scholarly life.[15]

And this, surely, is part of the problem with the Revolution on film. Successful films count on and burnish at least partial knowledge of the Civil War, which lives on powerfully, viscerally, in American culture.[16] World War II is only just passing from living memory; Vietnam will reside there for decades to come. The Revolution has no such engines of memory and culture behind it, which also means no ready-made audience.

Feature-film directors force themselves to teach—to act as documentarians—in part because it's impossible to presume common knowledge of a complex, long-ago conflict, especially when the instructional energies devoted to it have been scant. High school American history surveys blow by the Revolution in a couple of weeks at most. At the college level, there are many times more offerings on the Civil War.[17] At all levels, most courses on the American founding teach the era's ideas—the war of the press and the pen—rather than its military, political, or social history.

Fifteen years ago, the American Revolution Center conducted a national survey of adult knowledge about the period, and the results were sobering: Nine in 10 of those surveyed thought they would pass a basic test about the period, and eight in 10 of them were wrong. "Americans highly value, but vastly overrate, their knowledge of the Revolutionary period and its significance," the History News Network reported, rather understating the case.[18]

The center has since become Philadelphia's insightful and dramatic Museum of the American Revolution. (Full disclosure: I served as a trustee of the museum.) But though the museum and many other civic institutions and educational projects are doing their level best to share the content, skills, and dispositions needed to create the memory that sustaining the Revolution's principles requires, the knowledge gap seems only to grow.

As measured by the National Assessment of Educational Progress (NAEP), student proficiency in US history is not only dismal but declining, with eighth graders nationwide scoring five points lower on average in 2022 than in 2018. Eighth-grade US history, for those who, like me, have deliberately blocked out all memory of that year, is typically when the founding era is taught. Twelve percent of students surveyed by the NAEP offered a proficient answer to the rights included in the Bill of Rights. Fewer than half could complete a matching exercise linking grievances as expressed in the Declaration of Independence to provisions for combating them in the Constitution. About the Revolution's causes and consequences, the NAEP did not even pose a question.[19]

"I was trying to make history readable, not obliterate it!" Alda's Burgess tells the movie-within-a-movie's tone-deaf director.

Comes the response: "Well, who really knows what happened a couple hundred years ago?"[20]

The Promise and Perils of 1776

"Screw historical accuracy! This day is costing us at least $300,000!!" shouts Bo Hodges (Saul Rubinek), the fictional director of *Sweet Liberty*'s film within a film, before shooting a battle scene. He reminds Alda's truth-holding Professor Burgess that successful movies need young audiences, and young audiences want to see a movie do three things: "Defy authority, destroy property, and take people's clothes off."[21]

The American Revolution featured all of those, of course. Still, the point is worth noting: A movie with no audience is, by definition, a failure. If people won't pay to see it, the producers and distributors lose money. And if they lose money, they're unlikely to reinvest in the subject.[22] The threshold for period dramas is higher; it's expensive to counterfeit the olden days.

Of course, so is the world-building required to bring fantasy epics such as *The Lord of the Rings* to life. Making the trilogy cost a reported $281 million. But the return on investment was stratospheric; globally, the three *Lord of the Rings* films grossed nearly $3 billion.[23]

What would it mean to create a $3 billion global market for films about the American Revolution? To ask the question is to ponder what cinema does well. It entertains by plunging us into predicaments that feel real, open-ended, and urgent. The question of *Apollo 13* (1995) is only superficially "Will the astronauts make it back alive?" Ron Howard's movie transcends time and place because it prompts questions that resonate with any viewer: Am I a leader or a follower? When, not if, the emergency arises, will I be equal to the task? Maybe even: What does it mean for a country and its people to dare great things by risking terrible mistakes?

The people and predicaments of the American Revolution not only can but *should* provoke humanistic questions of this sort. Flawed heroes abound. Monticello's Jefferson—the guy who wrote the thing, as we call him in these parts—was America's enduring vernacular philosopher of liberty who enslaved more than 610 people over his lifetime, all the while knowing that slavery was a profound moral wrong. I'd watch that biopic, especially if Damian Lewis played Jefferson. Excellent source material proliferates. If Lin-Manuel Miranda could tease *Hamilton* from Ron Chernow's doorstop biography, imagine what Steven Spielberg could do with Annette Gordon-Reed's *The Hemingses of Monticello*. Imagine the biopic in which (Lewis's) Jefferson was, in the end, only one among many founders. That would be good history, good cinema, and—dare I say it?—good for America.

But it would be no simple matter to achieve. Hugh Hudson's *Revolution* (1985), starring Al Pacino, surely represents one of the worst investments of time, talent, and treasure in film history, if not in US history. Hudson, an Etonian who knew his way around a war picture, had breakthrough success with *Chariots of Fire* (1981), for which he received an Oscar nomination and won a slew of BAFTAs. What possessed him to tackle Britain's American War, much less to cast Pacino, fresh from *Scarface* (1983), in the lead, is a question better fit for a psychologist than a historian.

The action begins in July 1776, when the Declaration of Independence is read aloud in New York City. (That this actually happened on July 9, and not, as the title tells us, July 4, is the most minor of problems against what follows.) Pacino, playing an illiterate backwoods boatman named Tom Dobb, pulls up to the wharves, looking for work. He finds instead trouble with a capital T, right there in East River city.

Swept into a righteous conflict, he finds only villains. The Tories are rouged fops. The British are sadistic pedophiles. The Patriots are desperate and unprincipled, press-ganging men and even boys (like Tom's suffering son) into the army. Even Washington takes up the lash, flogging wounded men back to the front lines. "*Government is the problem*," joked one Monticello staffer. It was definitely not morning in Hudson's Ronald Reagan–era fantasy of American beginnings.

The film's failures of pace, plot, character, and scene are too numerous to count. Suffice to say that the English county of Devon makes a poor stand-in for Yorktown.[24] The viewer has no idea what this cruel war is over, though Dobbs makes mention in the final frames of heading west to "find us a place . . . where there ain't nobody better than you."[25]

On screen, there ain't nobody worse: Pacino is, in a word, dire, his gelled coif in full '80s glory even amid the filth of flight and battle, his character less stable than his accent, which bounces from Bonnybridge to Bensonhurst and back, sometimes in a single sentence. *New York*'s David Denby compared the performance to "Chico Marx with a head cold."[26] The actor later told his authorized biographer that the film had been released incomplete, suggesting that "more cutting—viewing the movie more as a silent film" might have saved the day.[27] More Harpo, less Chico.

The makers of *Revolution* went big and went home far poorer than they started. Could they throw it over their shoulder like a Continental soldier? They could not. From a budget of $28 million (more than $80 million in 2025 dollars), *Revolution* grossed less than $400,000.[28]

The emptiness at the film's core, comments Brandon Dillard, who directs Monticello's historic interpretation, is the absence of story. A historical film is like the journey through a historic site. "No amount of content knowledge can make a good tour, but a great story will," Dillard notes. *Revolution* had flags—really good flags!—and extras aplenty, but the plot lacked the narrative arc to sustain even a trailer. On Rotten Tomatoes, *Revolution* has earned the rare distinction of a score of 10 . . . on a scale from one to 100.[29]

After *Revolution* bombed, Pacino went to ground for several years. "It was that single film that took the rug out from under me," he recalled.[30] The critic Leonard Maltin predicted that such a "mega-bomb" augured ill for the future. "Only a half-dozen or so movies have dealt more than superficially with the Revolutionary War." He predicted that "it'll be 2776 until we get another."[31]

It took only 15 years till the disaster movie magnate Roland Emmerich, fresh off the global success of the intergalactic action film *Independence Day* (1996), decided to pursue the story of an independence battle much closer to home. Columbia Pictures invested over $110 million in *The Patriot* (2000), starring Mel Gibson, who had cut his blinding white teeth on battle pictures both imperial (*Gallipoli* and *Braveheart*) and cosmic (*Mad Max*).[32] In addition to enlisting a star-studded cast, Emmerich commissioned a score from John Williams, which has the resonance and the drive of Aaron Copland on acid.

As history, *The Patriot* is wretched, bearing the same relationship to the colonial past as *Godzilla* does to herpetology, as the historian David Hackett Fischer quipped.[33] The most noxious of its failures of fact include the script's treatment of the non-white population. The action takes place almost entirely in South Carolina, a colony more deeply implicated in the plantation nexus than any other on the mainland. Yet its black population—which constituted the majority of its residents—is portrayed as fulfilled, self-determining, and, at least in the household of our protagonist, Benjamin Martin (Gibson), free, which would have been anomalous if not illegal in the revolutionary period. The plot extols the derring-do of militiamen who answer to nobody and deprecates the effectiveness of Continental soldiers who play by the rules of war, a choice at odds with American history and one striking indeed in a movie released only five years after the carnage Timothy McVeigh inflicted on federal workers and their children in the Oklahoma City bombing.

As over-the-top action, *The Patriot* partly succeeds. Emmerich keeps the focus tightly on Martin and his family. Gibson brings the sword-swinging, axe-wielding, whites-of-his-eyes energy he displayed several years earlier in *Braveheart* (1995), absent the blue paint and with the addition of a low-slung ponytail. There is no ambiguity at all about the nature of the enemy. The Patriots are Good, colonials who ally with the Crown are Bad, and the British themselves are Worst, either bloodthirsty sadists or sniveling placemen not even a dog can respect. Martin's alienation of the affection of two Great Danes owned by General Charles Cornwallis offers some of the picture's scant comic relief. Even when the action strains credibility, it's a good bet to root for the man whom dogs love, especially if he can swing a mean tomahawk.

And root audiences did: Whatever else can be said about Emmerich's imagined past, it repaid its producers' considerable investment, grossing more than $215 million, nearly half of that outside the United States.[34] A singular accomplishment for an industry where freedom is anything but free.

Where *Revolution* and *The Patriot* reveal the challenges and opportunities of cinematic maximalism, Peter H. Hunt's *1776* (1972), the filmed version of the 1969 Tony Award–winning theatrical musical by Peter Stone and Sherman Edwards, showcases the power of a focused minimalism inherent in the genre of filmed play. Both time and space are tightly controlled—a bottle episode. The action takes place almost entirely in one room in Philadelphia's Independence Hall in June 1776. Characters unfurl themselves quickly through song and silence: the obnoxiousness of Adams ("Sit Down, John"), the braggadocio of Richard Henry Lee ("The Lees of Old Virginia"), the cold calculation of enslaver Edward Rutledge ("Molasses to Rum"), and the uxoriousness of both Adams ("Till Then" and "Yours, Yours, Yours") and Jefferson ("He Plays the Violin").

Dramatists and historians alike can learn a good deal from the synoptic qualities of musicals. A leitmotif may be a biographer's best friend. Yet while controlling the scene of the action, Hunt, Stone, and Edwards allow dispatches from the outside world—literal dispatches. Abigail writes to John. A nameless courier from the Continental Army, the rare common man in a roomful of dandies, pops in to declaim letters from Washington, taking us into the bloody fields and the starving encampments. Each of his messages concludes with "Your obedient [snare drum], *G. Washington*," returning us to Congress's knowledge of what's happening beyond the fourth wall and why it matters. The courier's power ballad, "Momma Look Sharp," reminds us that war, even bewigged 18th-century war, is hell.

1776 is imperfect as both play and cinema. It's talky, with a great deal of debate and much less singing than a typical musical, 11 numbers to *Hamilton*'s 46. It has pacing problems, including one of the longest first acts in the history of musical theater. The cast—those 56 men battling it out in Congress—represents only the merest sliver of the 2.5 million people of the rebellious 13 colonies, all of whom, in their varied and often opposed ways, were founders of the United States.[35] But by gosh and by golly, we know what the fight is about, both the war for home rule and the war for who will rule at home. We can sense the tensions of the future:

the cleavages of race, condition, and section that would roil the nation for generations and roil it still.

Yet Hunt, like Stone and Edwards before him, is confident in his powers of synecdoche: making a part stand in for the whole. Without synecdoche, historical cinema becomes mere visual encyclopedia. In *Glory*, we allow Colonel Robert Gould Shaw and the brave, doomed men of the 54th Massachusetts to represent the tensions within the North and between North and South, the moral arc of the Civil War, and indeed the vicissitudes of War Itself, all in a tight two hours.

War pictures across a wide swath of time and space harness the power of synecdoche as few other genres do. The brigade, the battle, the camp, the casualty, the grunt, the general, the sadistic commandant—each is offered, with profound moral clarity, as a grain of sand that contains dizzying worlds. The formula works outside the United States and across the broad sweep of American history. Think *All Quiet on the Western Front* (1930) or even the ultimate battle-bottle episode, *Das Boot* (1981). But in too many American Revolution movies, we are everywhere, everyone, all at once. What makes the Revolution so relatively immune to a timeworn storytelling formula?

Who Is This "We, the People"?

As in its later cinematic incarnations, the history of the American Revolution resists easy narration. Its middle and ending are as murky as its beginnings. And its epic cast is hard to get a handle on. For the North America of the founding generation consisted of myriad separate countries—Adams called Massachusetts his country, as Jefferson did Virginia—with a bewildering range of subjects in each of them. Adams alluded to the polyglot polity when he told Niles that it had been "a Singular Example in the History of Mankind" when "Thirteen Clocks were made to Strike together; a perfection of Mechanism which no Artist had ever before effected."[36]

Adams underestimated the complexity of the mechanism as radically as he exaggerated the convergence that had been achieved. Britain's America included 26 clocks, half of which remained in the empire when all was said and done. In the confederated 13, between one-fifth and one-third of the population remained loyal to the Crown. Some 60,000 to 80,000 of those fled the new United States, the rough equivalent of several million Americans today.[37] Anywhere from one-third to two-fifths of the population were, in the words of their countrymen, "wavering," "disaffected," or "flexible"—neutrals, inconstant, and often despised. At the onset of the war, consistent Patriots—the *we* of the cinematic universe—represented no more than 40 percent of the rebellious colonies' population. The American Revolution was a war of colonial liberation, a civil war, and an imperial war all in one.

And that's just loyalty. The picture grows more tessellated still when we dig into demography. More than 50 percent of the population was female. A disproportionate number were children, as in all developing nations. One-fifth were enslaved, some 500,000 men, women, and children.[38] Their political loyalties followed their personal and familial quests for life, liberty, and happiness, which led most often in the direction of the Crown.

Poorer colonials fought beside, as well as against, those who claimed to be their betters. Westering farmers had dramatically different priorities than the Eastern moneyed men who comprised a tiny sliver of the population and an enormous proportion of the legislatures of their states. In the vast interior of the continent—Indian country—several hundred Native nations made their own choices and took their own chances to preserve the *inter*dependence that had sustained them for centuries, if not millennia.

The French diplomat J. Hector St. John de Crèvecoeur's famous 1782 question "What is an American?" gets its weight, then as now, from being so damnably difficult to answer.[39] Crèvecoeur wrote when a common political identity was coming into focus; the Treaty of Paris, then in draft, gave the people of the United States at least paper coherence. In 1776, even a provisional response to his query would have been hard to sketch. Nor were the nature and character of the enemy all that much clearer, given the involvement of Native tribes, Hessian soldiers, and Canadian colonials who fought alongside the British. As one of my Monticello colleagues noted, the American Civil War, for all its complexity, was a cleaner, clearer, and geographically much tighter conflict.

The dizzying pluralism of the would-be nation's populace was also spread over an unfathomably large and varied geography, across which rapid information sharing was impossible—a factor in the war's conduct in the 18th century and its dramatizations in the present day. A question asked in Boston, needing a reply from Parliament in London, took five or six months to complete the circuit. The situation in the British American colonies was speedier, but not by much. From Griffith's *America* to Emmerich's *The Patriot*, directors of films set in the revolutionary era have leaned on postriders to inch the news from place to place in a desperate attempt to make it plausible that people in western New York or Virginia or South Carolina knew much and cared more about the plight of Boston.

Several generations of recent scholarship have worked heroically to muddy the waters still further. The last major attempt at a scholarly yet driving narrative synthesis of the war was Robert Middlekauff's *The Glorious Cause*, published in 1982.[40] In the intervening decades, diligent scholars, including yours truly, have recovered unsung protagonists, surfaced overlooked perspectives, and excavated tensions within the American populace. We have humanized the Loyalists, ferreted out the shape-shifting neutrals, and complicated the Patriots, from whose paradoxes we cannot and should not turn away.

Even Washington, the indispensable man in the winning of the United States, was a deeply complicated figure. For his exterminating strategy against the Crown's Native allies in western New York, the Seneca nicknamed him *Conotocarius*, or "town destroyer."

In recent historiography, the cause is no longer glorious nor even common. We have, in the most towering recent synthesis, many and various and often conflicting American Revolutions, intersecting in unpredictable ways, across a vast and divided continent, without a country in sight.[41] The pixelated picture is more accurate; we need to hold *all* these truths to successfully hold any. But all this *e pluribus pluribus* does not an easy cinematic triumph make.

Was it ever thus? I was struck, watching this run of films, by how long directors and their underlying source material, consisting chiefly of justly forgotten novels, have wrestled with cleavages *within* the rebel American population. Both Ford's *Drums Along the Mohawk* and Frank Lloyd's *The Howards of Virginia* get their energy from the tension between honest backwoods yeomen and sneering coastal elites. These are productions, in other words, about what the historian Carl Lotus Becker back in 1909 posed as "the question, if we may so put it, of who should rule at home."[42]

In both films, earnest lower-middling strivers marry well-born women from families who find their daughters' love matches both preposterous and dangerous. Gilbert Martin, Henry Fonda's character in *Drums Along the Mohawk*, snags an elegant Albany bride and promptly spirits her away into the primeval forests of the Mohawk Valley. The war over home rule is distant from this frontier, where pidgin-speaking Iroquoians wander into log cabin living rooms. There's some discussion among Martin's neighbors about a distant conflict over making people pay taxes in which they have no say. But the general message is one of bootstrapping citizen can-do-ism: "Congress can't help us.... We have to look after ourselves."[43]

Young Matt Howard, protagonist of *The Howards of Virginia*, hails from western Albermarle County, along the Blue Ridge. A fish out of water in refined Williamsburg even as a schoolboy, he battles his Latin tutor and dreams of "Ohio, where men can be free!" He returns to the colonial capital as Cary Grant in buckskins, a majestic bull in the porcelain shop of refined salons and genteel gambling. His boyhood friend, Jefferson, gets him in a bathtub and outfits him in the proper duds to make the connections that will allow him to succeed as a surveyor of western lands, which, after all, had been good enough for Washington. But Howard can't stand "the constarn things"; he's a big-boned rustic distrustful of "manners"—a natural American when push comes to shove.[44]

Both *Drums Along the Mohawk* and *The Howards of Virginia* were filmed on the eve of America's entry into World War II, which made casting Britain as the enemy of American freedom impossible. In Ford's Oriskany epic, we see no redcoats, only "savage Indians" and their loyalist allies in footage that might well have been retrieved from the cutting-room floor of *Stagecoach*, released the same year. The war Martin and his neighbors experience is a polygonal conflict of all against all, a conflict without ideology—a frontier guerrilla war.

"That's our new flag, the thing we've been fighting for," the Continentals tell the shivering inhabitants of a depleted American fort when they come through to say the war is over.[45] But it doesn't quite ring true. Despite the film's blatant attempt to "stoke the American spirit," as one of my colleagues from the Papers of Thomas Jefferson project said during our watch party, Ford leaves us without a clear understanding of what that spirit is or does.

In *The Howards of Virginia*, too, the enemy is right here at home, in the form of the coastal aristocracy and its anglicized ways, including chattel slavery. The genteel Peytons, the Cavalier clan into which Howard marries, are as remarkable for their prejudices as for their refinement. "You didn't actually labor in the fields?" an appalled Miss Jane Peyton (Martha Scott) asks Grant's Howard. "I thought only . . ." Her voice trails away, picturing the work of enslaved men on her father's Elm Hill plantation.[46]

Howard has represented himself as an expert surveyor, which is wishful at best; Jefferson is accused of having presented him to the family "under false colors," given that he's "nothing but poor white." When Howard asks Fleetwood Peyton, the tidewater patriarch whose worldview is as crippled as his right leg, for his sister's hand, Fleetwood rejoins, "Do you mean she should go to Ohio, and follow you like a squaw?!"[47] Howard means precisely that—the source of both the movie's drama and its comedy.

It seems surprising, given the growth of the scholarly fields of African American history and studies, that slavery figures more largely in *The Howards of Virginia* than it has in any American Revolution movie since. Black actors have named speaking roles as members of the Howards' enslaved workforce. Their subjectivity is not deeply plumbed; they carry the ideals and the burdens of those who claim to own them. Dicey, Jane Peyton's enslaved ladies' maid, has no patience for the leveling worldview of her mistress's new husband and wants to take her mistress out of the backcountry. "You could love a man till you're fit to bust," Dicey says, "but no lady of quality could make out here."[48]

To modern ears, the effect is uncomfortably like the role of Butterfly McQueen as Miss Prissy in *Gone with the Wind*, released the year before *The Howards of Virginia*. Yet Dicey and her kin are not invisible. And there is the intimation that their day will come. "What's the good of independence if we don't use it to build a new system that's fair to all?" Jefferson asks Howard before writing the thing that started it all.[49] What good indeed?

The Problem of Endings

It's hard to end an essay, and it must be tougher still to wrap a movie, what with all the sets and the trailers and the catering trucks needing to be set to rights. Even so, it's striking that all but one of the movies discussed here faces a disastrous time fading to black. For nearly a hundred years, filmmakers have insisted on fast-forwarding, by hook and often by crook, to the end of the war and beyond, no matter how big the time bump involved.

Though its core battle takes place in 1777, Ford can't holler, "CUT!" in *Drums Along the Mohawk* till Continentals straggle onto the scene five or six years later. *The Howards of Virginia*, too, jumps from the Valley Forge winter of 1777 to Yorktown in 1781 as if possessing Harry Potter's time-turner. *The Patriot* likewise trudges on to Cornwallis's defeat, with the British general played by the late, great Tom Wilkinson sputtering a line worse than his battle tactics: "Everything has changed." *Revolution* ricochets forward to the evacuation of New York in 1783, and please, I beg you, don't make me rewatch the film to figure out how we got there.

Hamilton catapults furthest of all, with Eliza Hamilton's swan song, "Who Lives, Who Dies, Who Tells Your Story," taking place at some indeterminate moment shortly before her own passing, at the age of 97, in 1854.

Maybe we should blame the NAEP scores: If few Americans know the basic outlines of the American Revolution's plot, maybe they need to be reminded that the upstarts won. Or perhaps the sheer improbability of that outcome makes it filmically irresistible to continue to the war's conclusion, as if Butch and Sundance peered out of their shack at the entirety of the Bolivian army and then miraculously prevailed.

Why not make the picture called *Yorktown*?[50] But that would mean the origin story is visible only in the distant rearview. And few filmmakers, it seems, are willing to pick one or the other bookend of a conflict that formally lasted eight years. The result is a whole shelf of nonsense.

The glorious exception is *1776*, which ends with Congress inking the script that formed the credal foundation of our peoplehood. (The bottle episode format forces compression even then; the signatories assemble at once on July 4 in the story, not by fits and starts into August as they did in reality.) We hear a (fictitious) dispatch from Washington explaining the overwhelming odds against the Continentals—a force of 5,000 older men and greenhorn boys—arrayed against five times as many British regulars. "How it will end only Providence can direct," his courier reads.[51] Everything hangs in the balance in the movie's gasp-inducing final frames, as the signers one by one take their places before dissolving into John Trumbull's famed and fanciful semicentennial painting. There is no fast-forward to Yorktown, booyah.

To leave us in medias res, as *1776* does, is to pass the burden of history and its living present to the audience—a republic, if you can keep it, as Franklin is alleged to have said. In a medium dedicated to entertainment, this surely is the essential move. Maybe historians could consider it too.

For the American Revolution is not over. Let Abigail Adams sing the point home: It's *yours, yours, yours.*

Notes

1. American Film Institute Catalog, "Bowling Green," https://catalog.afi.com/Film/41338-BOWLING-GREEN.

2. Mike Fleming Jr., "Disney Paid $75 Million for Worldwide Movie Rights to Lin-Manuel Miranda's 'Hamilton'; Biggest Film Acquisition Deal Ever?," *Deadline*, February 3, 2020, https://deadline.com/2020/02/disney-paid-75-million-hamilton-movie-deal-lin-manuel-miranda-largest-film-acquisition-ever-1202849929/.

3. See the advertisement for *The Spy* in *The Billboard*, May 30, 1914, 52, Internet Archive, https://ia801909.us.archive.org/BookReader/BookReaderImages.php?id=sim_billboard_1914-05-30_26_22&itemPath=%2F12%2Fitems%2Fsim_billboard_1914-05-30_26_22&server=ia801909.us.archive.org&page=leaf00053.

4. Wilson probably didn't say it, per Mark E. Benbow, "Birth of a Quotation: Woodrow Wilson and 'Like Writing History with Lightning,'" *The Journal of the Gilded Age and Progressive Era* 9, no. 4 (2010): 509–33, http://www.jstor.org/stable/20799409.

5. Todd McCarthy, "The Patriot," *Variety*, June 16, 2000, https://variety.com/2000/film/reviews/the-patriot-2-1200462809/.

6. John Adams to Hezekiah Niles, February 13, 1818, Founders Online, https://founders.archives.gov/documents/Adams/99-02-02-6854.

7. Thomas Jefferson, *A Summary View of the Rights of British America* (Williamsburg, VA, 1774).

8. Wanting to think about narrative conventions within a standard cinematic time frame is my excuse for sweeping prestige TV serial dramas like *John Adams* and even *Turn: Washington's Spies* off the stage here.

9. *America*, directed by D. W. Griffith (D. W. Griffith Productions, 1924).

10. *Drums Along the Mohawk*, directed by John Ford (Twentieth Century Fox, 1939).

11. *The Howards of Virginia*, directed by Frank Lloyd (Frank Lloyd Productions and Columbia Pictures, 1940).

12. *The Time of Their Lives*, directed by Charles Barton (Universal Pictures, 1946).

13. Like, a lot.

14. *Sweet Liberty*, directed by Alan Alda (Universal Pictures, 1986).

15. Sing it, brother. I still remember the cocktail party, in the 1980s, when I told some business folk that I studied 17th-century New England. "You mean, like, Cotton Mather???" Indeed.

16. American culture where—spoiler alert—the South won.

17. There is no easy way to get reliable data, but searching for courses with "American Revolution" or "Civil War" in their titles on CollegeTransfer.Net, which tells college transfer applicants where they might find courses on subjects of interest, offers a reasonable kludge. AcademyOne, CollegeTransfer.Net, website, https://www.collegetransfer.net/.

18. History News Network, "American Revolution Center Releases National Survey Results: 83 Percent of U.S. Adults Fail Test on Nation's Founding," December 3, 2009, https://www.historynewsnetwork.org/article/american-revolution-center-releases-national-surve.

19. National Assessment of Educational Progress, "NAEP Report Card: U.S. History," https://www.nationsreportcard.gov/ushistory/results/scores/. For questions, see National Assessment of Educational Progress, Questions Tool, https://www.nationsreportcard.gov/nqt/searchquestions.

20. *Sweet Liberty*, directed by Alda.

21. *Sweet Liberty*, directed by Alda.

22. For a generation, we've seen this principle operate in reverse, in the growth of the Marvel and DC Comics cinematic universes: If it packs the theaters, make it again.

23. Eammon Jacobs, "'The Lord of the Rings' Made Almost $3 Billion at the Box Office—so You Might Be Surprised by How Much Its Actors Got Paid," *Business Insider*, September 17, 2024, https://www.businessinsider.com/lord-of-the-rings-cast-salaries-pay-2024-9.

24. Benedict Nightingale, "A Yankee Revolution in England," *The New York Times*, July 14, 1985, https://www.nytimes.com/1985/07/14/movies/a-yankee-revolution-in-england.html.

25. *Revolution*, directed by Hugh Hudson (Goldcrest Films International and Viking Films, 1985).

26. Denby quoted in David Wolf, "Pacino: Master of the Method," *Financial Review*, May 9, 2014, https://www.afr.com/politics/pacino-master-of-the-method-20140314-ixkws.

27. *Al Pacino: In Conversation with Lawrence Grobel*, ed. Lawrence Grobel (Gallery Books, 2006), 182–83.

28. The Numbers, "Revolution (1985)," Nash Information Services, https://www.the-numbers.com/movie/Revolution.

29. Rotten Tomatoes, "Revolution," https://www.rottentomatoes.com/m/1028715-revolution.

30. *Al Pacino*, 182–83.

31. Leonard Maltin, *Leonard Maltin's 2001 Movie and Video Guide* (Plume, 2001), 1169.

32. *The Patriot*, directed by Roland Emmerich (Columbia Pictures, 2000).

33. Fischer, quoted in Thomas Doherty, "At Last, Our Revolution Done Right," *The Boston Globe*, July 16, 2000, E2.

34. Box Office Mojo, "The Patriot," IMDbPro, https://www.boxofficemojo.com/release/rl3244918273/weekly/?ref_=bo_rl_tab#tabs.

35. I have written elsewhere at some length about *1776*. See Jane Kamensky, "The *1776* Project," October 13, 2022, *The Atlantic*, https://www.theatlantic.com/ideas/archive/2022/10/1776-musical-broadway-founding-fathers/671717/.

36. Adams to Niles, February 13, 1818.

37. Maya Jasanoff, *Liberty's Exiles: American Loyalists in the Revolutionary World* (Alfred A. Knopf, 2011), 357.

38. See, for instance, US Census Bureau, *A Century of Population Growth from the First Census of the United States to the Twelfth*, 1790–1900, June 1909, https://www.census.gov/library/publications/1909/decennial/century-populaton-growth.html.

39. J. Hector St. John de Crèvecoeur, "Letter III—What Is an American," in *Letters from an American Farmer* (London, 1782), https://avalon.law.yale.edu/18th_century/letter_03.asp.

40. Robert Middlekauff, *The Glorious Cause: The American Revolution, 1763–1789* (Oxford University Press, 1982).

41. In Robert G. Parkinson's *The Common Cause*, the revolutionary cause is made common only by summoning racial rhetorics against black and Native Americans. Robert G. Parkinson, *The Common Cause: Creating Race and Nation in the American Revolution* (Omohundro Institute, 2016). See also Alan Taylor, *American Revolutions: A Continental History, 1750–1804* (W. W. Norton, 2016).

42. Carl Lotus Becker, *The History of Political Parties in the Province of New York, 1760–1776* (University of Wisconsin, 1909), 22.

43. *Drums Along the Mohawk*, directed by Ford.

44. *The Howards of Virginia*, directed by Lloyd.

45. *Drums Along the Mohawk*, directed by Ford.

46. *The Howards of Virginia*, directed by Lloyd.

47. *The Howards of Virginia*, directed by Lloyd.

48. *The Howards of Virginia*, directed by Lloyd.

49. *The Howards of Virginia*, directed by Lloyd.

50. The brilliant historian Kathleen DuVal is working on a new book about Yorktown. Maybe the movie will follow.

51. *1776*, directed by Peter H. Hunt (Columbia Pictures, 1972).

3

Americans and Their Revolution: The First 100 Years

ALLEN C. GUELZO

"Yesterday the 4th of July," announced the newspaper, "being the Anniversary of the Independence of the United States of America, was celebrated in this city with demonstrations of joy and festivity." Each of the "armed ships and gallies in the river [was] . . . dressed in the gayest manner, with the colours of the United States and streamers displayed," and at one o'clock, all gun crews onboard began firing "a discharge of thirteen cannon from each of the ships." There was a dinner for members of Congress, Army officers, and even "strangers of eminence," all followed by toasts "breathing independence, and a generous love of liberty" and more banging of artillery.[1]

It was, all in all, quite a "celebration," especially considering that it was the *first* ever such celebration—it was July 4, 1777—and took place in Philadelphia, which in less than three months would be occupied by an unforgiving British army. But at least for that moment, "there was a grand exhibition of fireworks (which began and concluded with thirteen rockets)." *The Pennsylvania Evening Post* solemnly hoped that "the fourth of July, that glorious and ever memorable day," would "be celebrated through America, by the sons of freedom, from age to age till time shall be no more."[2]

Judging strictly by the numbers, the *Evening Post* would probably be gratified by how energetically we have carried on those fiery celebrations of America's independence. In 2024, the American Pyrotechnics Association estimated that 16,000 professional fireworks shows lit up the nighttime skies across the nation on July 4. Just as fiery in their own way,

Coney Island held its annual hot-dog-eating contest, Philadelphia hosted its Pomp & Parade on Independence Mall, and the Boston Pops performed its annual Independence Day concert on the Charles River Esplanade, featuring the usual cannonade that accompanies Pyotr Ilyich Tchaikovsky's *1812 Overture*.[3]

But despite the exuberance, there is still some question about how bright a line should be drawn between 1777's hope that independence would be thereafter celebrated as "glorious" and the way it is actually done two and a half centuries later. The *1812 Overture* was, after all, written in honor of nothing more than the triumph of one absolutism (the Russian imperial one) over another (Napoleon's), representing the diametric opposites of what the American revolutionaries thought they were doing.

The African American Museum in Philadelphia featured a reenactment of Frederick Douglass's skeptical inquiry, "What to the Slave Is the Fourth of July?"[4] If anything, it has now become much more conventional, even among professional historians, to speak of the American Revolution not as the work of "the sons of freedom" but as "an internal civil war of extraordinary violence, justified by the rhetoric of a country in peril and folded into . . . a terror erupting with particular force . . . by white revolutionaries on Tories, on local white minorities, and on African and Native Americans," but then "crowded out of the master narrative by invocations of 'The Glorious Cause.'"[5] Perhaps such skepticism about the Revolution is the product of living in skeptical times, when institutions and narratives of every sort have surrendered much of their persuasive power to arguments that reduce all human events to unpleasant questions of power—in the spirit, we should say, of François de La Rochefoucauld's reduction of virtue to "nothing but" (*il n'y a rien*) or Michel Foucault's preference for "pessimistic activism."[6] As the historian Paul Finkelman has written, the loss of historical nuance has created a blind eye to how indifference and even hostility could exist side by side in the young United States, with admonitions to treat the Native tribes fairly and the first movements in the world to end slavery by public legal enactment.[7]

Our modern struggles to remember 1776 stand in vivid contrast to not only the observances in Philadelphia in 1777 but also the recollections of an earlier American historian, George Bancroft, who wrote as a student at the University of Göttingen in 1820, "Oh! My countrymen, never was a land blessed of heaven like ours. . . . My countrymen, we are Americans. The arts and sciences of Europe cannot make us forget it."[8] Far from understanding the American Revolution as a domestic tug-of-war over privilege and oppression, Abraham Lincoln spoke in 1861 of the "battle-fields and struggles for the liberties of the country" as an emblem of "a great promise to all the people of the world to all time to come."[9] Although Americans had come to disagree over the Declaration of Independence's meaning by Lincoln's time, for a century they largely treated the Revolution as a glorious event worth commemorating through public celebrations, monuments, primers, and political rhetoric.

Political Ritual

Strains of criticism have long inflected America's recollections of its revolutionary birth. Douglass's famous question on the platform of Corinthian Hall in Rochester, New York, in 1852 was not an exercise in cynical fatalism. It was a frank exposure of a great default on the Revolution's promises, which, as Douglass insisted to his audience of white New Yorkers, "brought life and healing to you" but "stripes and death to me" and to millions of others born, like Douglass, in slavery.[10] Similarly, Lincoln was painfully candid in 1855 when he admitted that, although "the fourth of July has not quite dwindled away" in significance, the spirit of freedom that Philadelphians saluted in 1777—"that spirit which desired the peaceful extinction of slavery"—had "itself become extinct, with the occasion, and the men of the Revolution" and had left the Fourth of July good for little more than "burning firecrackers!!!"[11]

Some of that ambivalence about the Revolution was in American minds almost from the nation's beginning. Sarah Logan Fisher, a Philadelphia

Loyalist who sat unhappily through the independence celebrations in 1777, thought of the revolutionaries as "an ungrateful set of men" who did not understand "the kindness & lenity" of British rule and who "still go on working their own destruction & will one day no doubt reap the reward of their works."[12]

And the revolutionary politicians were not at all gentle in respecting the pursuit of happiness when it was pursued by Loyalists like Fisher. In fact, Fisher's husband was one of 20 prominent Philadelphia Quakers denounced as traitors and thrust into exile without trial by Pennsylvania's revolutionary government. Her neighbor and fellow Loyalist, Elizabeth Drinker (whose husband had also been forced to join the other Quaker exiles), also noticed sarcastically how "the anniversary of Independence and Freedom" had been marked by vandalism of Quaker-owned shops, while Quaker residences had "a great number of windows broke."[13]

But Loyalism was a minority voice, and even more to the point, it lost. That allowed the revolutionaries free rein, over the first few decades of the new republic, to cast the Revolution in terms of almost redemptive glory. "It seems to have been reserved to the people of this country," wrote Alexander Hamilton in the first of the Federalist Papers, that they should "by their conduct and example . . . decide the important question, whether societies of men are really capable or not, of establishing good government from reflection and choice."[14]

In the generation that stretched from 1776 until 1826, Americans believed (according to David Ramsay, the first historian of the Revolution) that the old colonists "were from their first settlement in America, devoted to liberty." They were of one mind "that God made all mankind originally equal" and "endowed them with the rights of life, property, and as much liberty as was consistent with the rights of others."[15]

Americans were also moved "by the consideration that they were no longer to risque their lives for the trifling purpose of procuring a repeal of a few oppressive acts of parliament, but for a new organization of government" that "led them to substitute the majesty of the people, in lieu of discarded royalty."[16] The Revolution was the "unanswerable and invulnerable bulwark of freedom, the Rights of Man." And from the 1790s onward, public readings of the Declaration of Independence on successive Fourths of July became a kind of American political ritual and a "definition of the rights of man."[17]

Events and Ideas

By the 1820s, the way the American Revolution was fixed in American memory had begun to diverge into two distinct objects of remembrance. One of these would be the Revolution itself, in which attention would be focused on celebrating the events and personalities of the revolutionary era, especially the Fourth of July. The other would fix on the ideas of the Revolution as captured in the Declaration of Independence. These were not necessarily exclusive. As the United States moved past the Revolution's 50th anniversary, it was not difficult to hear these two voices sometimes singing in harmony but also sometimes solo.

Monuments to battles of the Revolution made their debut comparatively late. Lexington installed a modest monument to its militia in 1799. Baltimore erected what may be the first large-scale revolutionary monument—a 178-foot column honoring George Washington—in 1809. John Trumbull's four celebratory depictions—of the signing of the Declaration of Independence, the battles of Saratoga and Yorktown, and Washington resigning his commission—were finished and hung in the Capitol Rotunda by 1826.[18]

But remembrances of the Revolution as a political event were well underway in other forms long before the turn was made to "monumentation." Massachusetts made the Fourth of July a state holiday in 1781, marked in Boston by an annual oration that continued until 1876. In 1798, members of Congress "and other citizens" sponsored a Fourth of July banquet at Fouquet's Tavern in Philadelphia. The toasts that went round saluted "National Independence"; "Republicanism, pure, genuine and elective"; and the Constitution—"may it be protected against unconstitutional laws, the fatal effects of a system of alarm, and the reign of terror"—which was clearly a swipe at John Adams's presidency and the Sedition Act.[19] On the other hand, the same 1798 celebrations of the Fourth in July in Dedham, Massachusetts, rejoiced over "the birthday of American independence" by honoring "our free republican constitution" and "liberty and good government" while lauding Adams—"may his country never deny him that reward, which will be bestowed by his conscience and a posterity"—precisely for signing and enforcing the Sedition Act.[20]

Very quickly, the Fourth of July became a signifier of the Revolution as a whole, since (as one 19th-century elementary schoolbook stated flatly) "on that day this country became a nation; it threw off the shackles of colonial dependence."[21] The holiday also came to reflect contemporary debates over the meaning of the nation whose birth it celebrated. In 1788, for example, anti-Federalist critics of the new Constitution used the Fourth of July to stage a public burning of a copy of the Constitution, which promptly provoked a street brawl with Federalists, armed with clubs and paving stones, "fighting with greatest rage, and determined obstinacy."[22]

During the War of 1812, New York Federalists used the anniversary of independence to jab their Democratic opponents in a slightly less violent form for bringing an unwelcome war down on their heads. They ironically toasted to "the Conquest of Canada," which had been undertaken by "our soldiers without clothing—The chief commander wanting in military skill—Our numbers inferior to the enemy"—all of which they hoped would make President James Madison "weep for his ill-timed expedition."[23] In 1845, one correspondent of an Ohio newspaper complained that "*party*, political party" had in the previous year "attempted . . . to turn the patriotism and hollowed associations of this great day to party aggrandizement."[24] (Emphasis in original.) (And there were moments when some Americans seemed willing to turn the Fourth on its head through their actions rather than their words, as John Marshall did on July 4, 1784, when he bought four slaves, and again on July 4, 1787, when he bought two more.)[25]

Still, whatever reservations some Americans harbored about Adams or Madison as presidents, in the half century that followed independence, there was little shadow cast on the achievement of the Revolution itself.[26] Some argued that the memory of the Revolution could even allay the animosities that had set Federalists and Democrats at each other's political throats at the turn of the 19th century.[27] A "grateful recollection" of the Revolution's issues should, argued Massachusetts Representative Edward Everett in 1833, have "a natural tendency to soften the harshness of party" and "unite the patriotic feelings of every American."[28] But even when the nation was torn apart by the Civil War, Lincoln interpreted the twin victories at Gettysburg and Vicksburg in July 1863 as a providential mark of solidarity with the revolutionary struggle, since "the cohorts of those who opposed the declaration that all men are created equal, 'turned tail' and ran" on the Declaration's anniversary.[29]

More than benefiting only Americans, the Revolution was also hailed as an international event. Thomas Paine thought it presaged an entirely "new method of thinking" in 1782. "We see with other eyes; we hear with other ears; and think with other thoughts, than those we formerly used," he concluded.[30] The Revolution spelled the end of "the institutions of the old world," claimed Brown University President Francis Wayland in 1833, so that "there can be no doubt that other governments, following our example, will be formed on the principles of equality of right."[31]

The Revolution was the great occasion that overthrew ancient habits of hierarchy. It demonstrated that liberty, not obedience, was the natural condition for human flourishing, and that alone made it an object of rejoicing for all who lived under tyranny. "When I anticipate . . . the future glory of my country," reflected Ramsay, "and the illustrious figure it will soon make on the theater of the world, my heart distends with generous pride for being an American." He continued,

> The tyrants and landlords of the Old World, who hold a great part of their fellow men in bondage because of their dependence for land, will be obliged to relax of their arbitrary

> treatment, when they find that America is an asylum for free-men from all quarters of the globe. . . . I am confident that the cause of America is the cause of Human Nature, and that it will extend its influence to thousands who will never see it, and procure them a mitigation of the cruelties and oppressions imposed by their arbitrary task-masters.[32]

"Yes," wrote the poet James Kirke Paulding in 1818,

> The bright day is dawning, when the West
> No more shall crouch before old Europe's crest,
> When men who claim thy birthright, liberty,
> Shall burst their leading strings and dare be free.
> Nor while they boast thy blessings, trembling stand,
> Like dastard slaves before her, cap in hand.[33]

Conversely, in 1804 some New York Federalists thought the Fourth of July might be high time to lay anti-British animosity to rest. They deplored the "reading or recital of the Declaration of Independence," with its fiery condemnation of the English king, as "at variance with the just and magnanimous sentiment which concludes the Declaration itself, that we hold '*our British Brethren*,' '*enemies in war*, IN PEACE FRIENDS.'"[34] (Emphasis in original.)

When the Marquis de Lafayette paid his 50th-anniversary visit to the United States in 1824, Pennsylvania Congressman Charles Ingersoll gave a speech marking the great and beneficent changes the Revolution had wrought. "The people have come to be treated with the respect of other sovereigns," Ingersoll declared, and through the example of the Revolution, "the political, intellectual, and physical state of man, is generally improved and improving." The gospel of the American Revolution, said Ingersoll,

> inculcates universal education; throws open all careers to all; superadds chemistry and natural philosophy to the arts of life,

> and political economy to the sciences of government; enacts laws by equal representation; simplifies their enforcement; restrains sparingly, punishes mildly; discourages hostilities, by leaving those to declare war who bear most of the brunt, and acquire least of the glory. Not that it pretends to remould humanity . . . but to give freer scope than heretofore to the doctrine, that . . . justice and moderation prevent wars; and that when they do occur, no military organisation can wage, abridge, or illustrate them like that patriotism, which thinks as well as feels.[35]

The Revolution could thus be celebrated both for what it had boldly achieved and for what it had wisely avoided. Monarchs and monarchists had boasted that "man was unable to govern himself," that a republic like the American one would be "tost by the violence of faction, corrupted by the intrigues of demagogues, or assailed by the sword of ambition" and would shortly force Americans "to undergo the same mutation of government which had overclouded the histories of Greece and Rome."[36] But Americans had taught them otherwise.

Celebrations of the revolutionary anniversary knew no geographical center. In 1813, the Georgian William Crawford, en route to France to serve as American diplomatic minister, jotted in his journal a description of a Fourth of July ceremony at sea, in which "the [crew], with clean Sunday clothes, were mustered, and the law of the United States read to them by their Commander."[37] A decade earlier, Meriwether Lewis and William Clark brought remembrance of the Revolution to the far side of the Mississippi for the first time on July 4, 1804, by firing one of their expedition's little swivel guns and naming a small stream Independence Creek.[38]

By 1845, remembering the Fourth throughout the West had become as formulaic as anything to be encountered in Boston, New York, or Philadelphia. In Cleveland, Independence Day began with a "salute upon the Square" by the local artillery company, which was "answered by a peal from the thirty-two pounder upon the hill . . . which waked the sleepiest in these burghs with its resounding echoes." The streets "were thronged with pedestrians," and the firemen paraded their engines "bearing a genuine live Eagle," followed by local militia companies and "the Leland's City Band." A public meeting assembled to hear a reading of the Declaration, followed by an oration, a 500-seat dinner, and the inevitable evening "pyrotechnic exhibition" at the courthouse of "Rockets, serpents and Roman candles," topped off by a balloon ascension.[39]

A few hundred miles to the west in Springfield, Illinois, locals followed an almost identical pattern: A procession was "formed at the First Presbyterian Church" with "Standard Bearers," "Young Ladies," and "Young Gentlemen," followed by a reading of the Declaration of Independence, an oration, and then "a dinner" and "toasts."[40]

There is a certain quaint lack of originality in many of these observances. But the very sameness of these events, like Everett's call for a revival of revolutionary unity, was a statement of national solidarity.

Primers in Liberty

The work of remembering the Revolution could not be confined solely to the anniversary of independence or monuments to its battles. "The events of our war of independence . . . should be familiar 'as household words,' to the mind of every child of liberty," declared the *Gazette of the United States* in 1826. "He should learn valour from Bunker's Hill . . . *endurance* of privations from the sufferers of Valley Forge—temperance in success from the victory of Yorktown—and patriotic devotion . . . from the master genius who guided them all," the *Gazette* counseled.[41] (Emphasis in original.) If he (or she) didn't, he would have no one to blame but himself, since the schoolbooks and primers of the early republic teemed with exaltations of the Revolution.

One New Jersey education advocate argued that while in America, where "almost every practical question of importance . . . mixes itself up in politics," it was "fortunate that education is one of those few questions on which men of all parties can and do meet." But this was only because in the most general sense, no one dissented from the view that the Revolution was fundamentally good.[42] "The love of liberty is natural to man," intoned John Russell's 1838 history textbook ("for the Use of Schools"), but Americans had inherited more than the usual share of it. "They had long cherished the republican principles which had carried them" across the Atlantic Ocean in the first place, and their victory in the Revolution was a universal warning "to those who, unmindful of the rights of the people, would lift against them the arm of power."[43]

Early republic educator Caleb Bingham posited that the Revolution created an "empire of freedom," and he prophesied in *The Columbian Orator*, a popular compilation of rhetoric for students, that it would "produce a revolution in morals as well as politics" around the globe.[44] Already, as Bingham noted in his companion schoolbook, *The American Preceptor*, "the whole European mind has undergone a revolution, neither confined to this or that country; but as general as the great causes which have given it birth, and still continue to feed its growth."[45]

Bingham also argued that the Revolution's intellectual influence extended to women: "Happily for the fair daughters of America, the thick mists of superstition and bigotry are vanishing away; and the sun of science begins to beam upon our land, and to irradiate the female mind." No wonder he could exhort "infant choirs, composed of male and female voices," to "join in praise of our political fathers." The words almost danced off Bingham's pages: "How transporting are the prospects of America! . . . Lo, a Ph[o]enix of empire rises from the ashes of the old world! . . . Here liberty has erected her standard, and bids defiance to despotism."[46]

It was no accident that Lincoln and Douglass took their earliest inspiration from such primers and preceptors.[47] And it was no accident either that when the immense crisis of the Civil War broke over Americans' heads, their instinct was to connect it to the Revolution. Lincoln repeatedly tied the campaign against slavery in the 1850s to the revolutionary example, arguing that slavery's opponents were "walking in the 'old paths' . . . of Washington."[48] He hoped that if the United States could contain the spread of slavery by placing it "where Washington and Jefferson and Madison placed it, it *would* be in the course of ultimate extinction." (Emphasis in original.) Americans would then be "fighting it in the Jeffersonian, Washingtonian, and Madisonian fashion."[49]

When Lincoln departed from his home in Springfield in February 1861 for his inauguration, he spoke of bearing a burden "greater than that which rested upon Washington." Ten days later, he again conjured the revolutionary example by telling the New Jersey Senate how much his youthful imagination had been stimulated by "the struggle here at Trenton, New-Jersey" in 1776 for "the liberties of the people."[50]

But Lincoln's most ambitious claim to revolutionary bona fides came the following day. Speaking on Washington's birthday at Independence Hall in Philadelphia, Lincoln explicitly linked his presidency to the principles of the Declaration of Independence: "All the political sentiments I entertain have been drawn, so far as I have been able to draw them, from the sentiments which originated, and were given to the world from this hall in which we stand." He had "pondered over the toils that were endured by the officers and soldiers of the army" and was willing to say, "If this country cannot be saved without giving up that principle, . . . I would rather be assassinated on this spot than to surrender it."[51]

Jefferson Davis, himself the son of a Revolutionary War veteran and the new president of the Confederacy, made a parallel claim to revolutionary connections, although on different grounds from Lincoln. The Confederacy "illustrate[d] the American idea that governments rest upon the consent of the governed, and that it is the right of the people to alter or abolish governments whenever they become destructive."[52] Davis chose Washington's birthday as the date for his formal inauguration in 1861, just a few weeks before Lincoln's. He took his oath standing at the base of an equestrian statue of Washington—a statue whose image became the iconic center of the Great Seal of the Confederacy.[53]

Lincoln and Davis were far from the only ones to link the Revolution with the secession crisis. "Another Bunker Hill is here—another revolution has begun," cried New York Representative John Cochrane to a "great mass meeting" of "one hundred thousand" on New York City's Union Square in April 1861. "You are the men to participate in that revolution; you are the men who are to decide its results," he thundered. (A chorus of voices shouted back, "We will do it.")[54]

On the day after Fort Sumter's surrender, the *Chicago Tribune* declared, "The blood which conquered at Bennington and Yorktown . . . has risen, to battle heat. Woe to those who encounter it in the just cause of defending the legacy of our first Revolution."[55] A day later, the *Tribune* added that "from one end of the land to the other the old fire of the Revolution is kindled, and millions of stout hearts are beating responsive to their country's call."[56]

One of Stephen Foster's last songs, "Nothing but a Plain Old Soldier," connected a nonagenarian's service in the Revolution, when "my home and my country to me were dear / And I fought for both when the foe came near," with the present demands of a new war:

> Again the battle song is resounding,
> And who'll bring the trouble to an end?
> The Union will pout, and Secession ever shout,
> But none can tell us now which will yield or bend.
> You've had many generals from over the land,
> You've tried one by one but you're still at a stand,
> But when I took the field we had one in command,
> Yet I'm nothing but a plain old soldier. . . .
> But I've handled a gun,
> Where noble deeds were done,
> For the name of my commander,
> Was George Washington.[57]

There is an eerie echo of this call of the Revolution in the diary of Philadelphian Alexander Wallace Givin, who found himself impelled to enlist in the Union army by a dream

> that Genl Washington appeared to me looking me in the eye said as he raised his hand in a solemn manner, "This country must and shall be free." Then vanished. When I awoke and told the dream to my wife, I said that means for me to go and fight for my country and my flag. My wife said "Go and God be with you."[58]

Givin enlisted the next day in the 114th Pennsylvania Volunteer Infantry.

A House Divided

Despite the distance between 18th-century political factions such as the Federalists and Anti-Federalists and 19th-century politicians such as Lincoln and Davis, few contested the importance of celebrating the Revolution and its happy and desirable consequences across the century after 1776. There was, for instance, no example of an American monarchist party, no serious proposals for resubmission to British rule, and no repudiations of the revolutionary leaders that anyone could get away with without the risk of tar and feathers.

The Declaration of Independence, by contrast, took on much more controversial weight. It became clear from the 1830s onward that the source of that division was slavery, the continuation of which half the country increasingly deplored and the other half was determined to justify. And since the Declaration's principles became the polestar of the abolition movement, proslavery forces had to somehow either diminish or reinterpret the Declaration to reconcile the meaning of the founding with legalized enslavement.

The conflict over the Declaration and its legacy might be said to have begun even before the Continental Congress adopted the document in 1776. Thomas Jefferson had originally included in the Declaration a denunciation of the slave trade (although not slavery itself) as a "cruel war against human nature itself, violating the most sacred rights of life and liberty in the persons of a distant people who never offended him"—only to have it removed by the congress to placate states with many slaveholders.[59]

Not that Jefferson did much to draw attention to this deletion. Although in 1774 he had declared that "the rights of human nature" had been "deeply wounded" by the transatlantic slave trade and that "the abolition of domestic slavery is the great object of desire in those colonies, where it was unhappily introduced in their infant state," the deleted portions of the Declaration are something of a high-water mark in Jefferson's personal decisions about slavery and the slaves he owned.[60] He was perfectly cognizant that slavery was a danger to the new republic, but less because it conflicted with his own statement in 1776—that "all men are created equal, that they are endowed by the Creator with certain inalienable Rights, and that among these are Life, Liberty, and the pursuit of Happiness"—and more because he feared the bloody consequences of any insurrection American slaves might stage for their own liberty. (The Declaration explicitly condemned the king for having "excited domestic insurrections amongst us.") As president, Jefferson was perfectly happy to sign the legislation that banned the importation of slaves in 1808, but he had nothing in view that looked toward abolishing slavery itself. He concerned himself mostly with avoiding an uprising similar to the one that had driven the French from Saint-Domingue (modern-day Haiti).

At his best, Jefferson would claim in 1820 that "the cession of that kind of property (for so it is misnamed) is a bagatelle which would not cost me a second thought"—if it could be done painlessly for slave owners. "But as it is," he continued, "we have the wolf by the ears, and we can neither hold him, nor safely let him go. Justice is in one scale, and self-preservation in the other." Hence, nothing.[61] (He made a similar comment—"we have the wolf by the ears"—to Lydia Sigourney in 1824, but that was about "Indian rights," not black slavery.) At his worst, Jefferson was (unlike his Federalist opponents) stupendously indifferent to the plight of Toussaint L'Ouverture and the black republicans of Haiti, a kind of personal Thermidor. Nor did he mind selling 85 slaves in the 1790s to pay for the French wines he had come to admire.[62]

Madison, who was the prime mover behind the Constitutional Convention, had long wondered whether emancipation "would certainly be more consonant to the principles of liberty."[63] Though the Madison family depended on slave labor, Madison himself hoped "to depend as little as possible on the labour of slaves."[64] When a slave who accompanied him to Congress in Philadelphia in 1783 refused to return with Madison to Virginia, Madison simply apprenticed him (for a fee) to a Philadelphia Quaker, since he could not "think of punishing him . . . merely for coveting that liberty for which we have paid the price of so much blood, and have proclaimed so often to be the right, & worthy the pursuit, of every human being."[65] This was still well short of emancipation, but it was far better than Jefferson's do-nothing-until-we-do-all approach.

There were many other Americans for whom the Revolution in general and the Declaration in particular made slavery increasingly and steeply unacceptable in the new republic. As early as 1780, *The New-Jersey Gazette* asked the Revolution's most logical question:

> While we are spilling our blood and exhausting our treasure in defence of our own liberty, it would not perhaps be amiss, to turn our eyes towards those of our fellow men now in bondage under us. We say, "all men are equally entitled to liberty and the pursuit of happiness" but are we willing to grant this liberty to all men?[66]

And if the Revolution alone didn't jog consciences on the subject, the juxtaposition of the American and Haitian revolutions did so for others. "If one treats the insurrection of the negroes as rebellion," asked one member of the Pennsylvania legislature in 1791, "what name can be given to that insurrection of Americans which secured their independence?"[67]

In postrevolutionary years, a ferment of emancipation continued to bubble. Massachusetts was the first, through a state constitutional provision and then a court decision, to remove legal protections for slavery. It was followed quickly by Pennsylvania, New Hampshire, Connecticut, Rhode Island, Vermont, New Jersey, and New York (although the abolition plans in Pennsylvania, New Jersey, and New York followed gradual timetables; in New Jersey, there were still 18 lifetime "apprentices" in the 1860 census).

The new national Congress created by the 1787 Constitution dealt with proposals to tax slave imports; suppress the slave trade; readopt the Northwest Ordinance, which banned slavery from new territories between the Ohio River and the Great Lakes (a law the Confederation Congress had originally passed in 1787); lay restrictions on transporting slaves to the Mississippi and Louisiana territories; and receive petitions to "undo the heavy bur[d]ens, and prepare the way for the oppressed to go free, that every yoke may be broken."[68] And Congress could do that because, as John Quincy Adams insisted in the debates over the Louisiana Purchase, "the Constitution does not recognize *slavery*—it contains no such word." To the contrary, "a great circumlocution of words is used merely to avoid the term *slaves*."[69] (Emphasis in original.) So it was by no means surprising to hear Robert Jefferson Breckinridge, a Kentucky politician turned Old School Presbyterian minister, agree that "slavery cannot endure" in the American atmosphere:

> The just, and generous, and enlightened hearts and minds of those who own the slaves will not allow the system to endure. State after state, the example has caught and spread—New-England—New-York—the Middle States on the seaboard; one after another have taken the question up, and decided it, all alike. The state of slavery is ruinous to the community that tolerates it, under all possible circumstances; and is most cruel and unjust to its victims. No community that can be induced to examine the question, will, if it be wise, allow such a canker

in its vitals; nor, if it be just, permit such wrong. We argue from the nature of the case, and the constitution of man.[70]

A Proposition of Dangerous Import

Breckinridge's sweet reasoning pointed to one way the new republic might ease away from the taint of slavery, even if he didn't exactly consider how the race of the emancipated slaves would enter into discussions of the equality promised in the Declaration of Independence. Instead, every rumor of slave insurrection froze the blood and hardened the hearts of slave owners like Jefferson, who was convinced that "if something is not done, and soon done, we shall be the murderers of our children"—without doing that obvious *something*.[71]

Even citizens of states that had ended slavery had no desire to see their commercial relations with slaveholders disturbed. And they had even less reason by the 1830s, when new technical developments in processing cotton made slave labor appear ideal for the cheap production of the Industrial Revolution's prime commodity. What was needed to ease slaveholders' pain at the unhappy collision of the Declaration and commercial profit was an ideological principle that would roll back the Declaration's confident description of all men as equal—and this was provided by the wave of toxic Romanticism that lapped up to America's Enlightenment shores.[72]

No one embodied Romantic politics more defiantly than South Carolina's John C. Calhoun. Calhoun went straight to the root of American political self-understanding by insisting that the Declaration, by taking inalienable natural rights as its fundamental premise, was an enormous mistake. "There had never been a proposition of such dangerous import, or which had been so misunderstood, or been productive of so much evil" as the notion that "certain inalienable rights" were natural to anyone, he argued. The notion of natural rights, distributed equally across the human species, was a mere "hypothetical truism," since "nothing can be more unequal than the quantum of liberty assigned to each individual."[73]

He asserted that liberty, for instance, is not an inherent right, hardwired into every individual, but "a reward to be earned, not a blessing to be gratuitously lavished on all alike." Some people, by Calhoun's estimate, were "too ignorant, degraded and vicious, to be capable either of appreciating or of enjoying it" and thus should not have liberty handed to them in any practical way.[74]

For Calhoun, the obvious example of "some people" was Africans and their enslaved descendants in America. For the "African race," slavery was not simply a labor system to which the power of nations had arbitrarily assigned it but "a positive good" that raised it up and bestowed as much in the way of blessing as it was capable of receiving. Until some sign appeared that "the black race" had moved beyond what Calhoun deemed ignorance, degradation, and viciousness, in slavery it must stay. "I hold [slavery] to be a good, as it has thus far proved itself to be," he asserted in 1837, "and will continue to prove so if not disturbed by the fell spirit of abolition."[75]

Calhoun believed that uneasy whites who appealed to the Declaration and its "created equal" language to condemn black slavery were simply fooling themselves. "If we trace it back," he declared before the Senate in 1848, "we shall find the proposition" about equality "expressed in the Declaration of Independence" had been "inserted in our Declaration of Independence without any necessity." According to Calhoun, the real origins of the American Revolution did not lie in any appeal to the Enlightenment's metaphysics but were instead evolutionary, as British colonists used, developed, and asserted traditional English liberties.[76]

In his telling, the impulse and objects of the Revolution shrank down to the dimensions of a fiscal dispute. Calhoun maintained that "breach of our chartered privileges, and lawless encroachment on our acknowledged and well-established rights by the parent country, were the real causes" of the Revolution, and these were "of themselves sufficient, without resorting to any other, to justify the step . . . in constructing the governments which were substituted in the place of the colonial."[77]

Like the European Romantics, history was for Calhoun an organic process, not a revelation of fixed natural law, and it emerged from the experience and emotional unities people in specific nations felt for each other, their customs, and their land. The American republic was simply a long-term outgrowth of English cultural identity, and it therefore was bound to reveal itself in new developments, in different places, and among the relations of different peoples by "slow and successive experience" for "correction and adaptation."[78]

Calhoun was particularly agitated from the 1820s onward by his resentment of the commercial possibilities that a republic of equal citizens might exploit to disadvantage an agricultural (and slave-owning) elite. The "manufacturing interest" was already beginning to "rear up a moneyed aristocracy" in America, he warned. Though Americans might at that moment see freedom and slavery as the primary national problem dividing "the manufacturing States" and "the Agricultural States," Calhoun (like David Ricardo, Thomas Malthus, and ultimately Karl Marx) foresaw that "the time will come when it will produce the same results between the several classes" and "the contest will be between the capitalists and operatives."[79]

The plantation system, by contrast, preserved what Calhoun imagined was a humane balance among labor, capital, and the environment. Every "plantation is a little community of itself," Calhoun believed, where generous-minded white men cared for contented and grateful black slaves in a quasi-medieval idyll. "Property in our slaves," he argued, "is but wages purchased in advance including the support and supplies of the laborers, which is usually very liberal." And "it ought to be a principle of morals and patriotism," he wrote to Edmund Ruffin in 1835, "that no gain is legitimate that does not leave the land as productive as it was before it was taken."[80]

The result, ironically, was that an imagined money oligarchy was replaced by an all-too-real slave oligarchy. Madison had feared this among the vices of the classical republics he had cataloged before the Constitutional Convention, warning, "In proportion as slavery prevails in a State, the Government, however democratic in name, must be aristocratic in fact."[81] Whereas a republic demands equality and equality ensures mobility, oligarchy is about hierarchy and stasis for all classes, free and slave alike. "Society is a pyramid," explained the placid editor of the *Nashville Daily Gazette* late in 1860. "We may sympathize with the stones at the bottom of the pyramid of Cheops, but we know that some stones have to be at the bottom, and that they must be permanent in their place."[82]

Calhoun was the most prominent voice questioning the Declaration of Independence's place in the American experience. Only slightly less mincing was the judgment of Henry St. George Tucker—a judge, member of Congress, and professor of law at Jefferson's alma mater, the College of William & Mary, and later at Jefferson's University of Virginia—who drew strict constitutional lines around what kind of independence the Declaration had actually fashioned. Colonies had already declared their independence individually and practically before the Declaration was even composed, Tucker argued, and from that moment, "all dependence on, and connexion with, Great Britain, absolutely and forever ceased." In fact, no declaration by the Continental Congress was even necessary; only "a decent respect for the opinions of mankind required a declaration of the causes, which impelled the separation . . . was proper to give notice of the event to the nations of Europe."[83]

What lay immediately behind this argument was the conviction that the states had staked out their own sovereignty before the collective declaration of July 1776, and they were thus entitled to resume it once slavery seemed to be under threat. The American Revolution and the Declaration were simply afterthoughts.[84] "The time must come," warned William & Mary history professor Thomas Roderick Dew in 1836, when slavery would rescue the nation from its outdated principles. "Domestic slavery, such as ours," he posited, "is the only institution which I know of, that can secure that spirit of equality among freemen, so necessary to the true and genuine feeling of republicanism."[85]

The zeal for "domestic slavery" finally pushed some Southerners into stating what most could not: that not only the Declaration but also the Revolution itself had been a vast mistake. In his infamous "Cornerstone

Speech" in March 1861, the Confederate vice president, Alexander H. Stephens, grasped the nettle most others had been unwilling to touch and denounced the entire revolutionary era for resting "upon the assumption of the equality of races." Unlike the Revolution, he argued, the Confederacy was "the first government ever instituted upon the principles in strict conformity to nature, and the ordination of Providence, in furnishing the materials of human society"—which, in a phrase, were the tenets of white supremacy.[86]

The revolutionary generation had failed to see this, but that failure was merely expected in the organic unfolding of history. "This truth has been slow in the process of its development," Stephens freely acknowledged, but "all truths are and ever . . . slow in development," and it had taken 85 years for racial dominance to be "admitted" as the true principle of government. It only made good evolutionary sense for Stephens to ask, "May we not, therefore, look with confidence to the ultimate universal acknowledgment of the truths upon which our system rests?"[87]

The doubts of Calhoun, Tucker, Dew, and finally Stephens generated a revulsion among antislavery activists, who were incredulous at the proposition that the Revolution had done nothing to promote either national unity or an end to slavery. Nothing seemed clearer to the Southern-born abolitionist Angelina Grimké in 1836 "that slavery is contrary to the declaration of our independence" and "reduces a *man* to a *thing*."[88] (Emphasis in original.) The black abolitionist Henry Highland Garnet described the Declaration to the National Convention of Colored Citizens in Buffalo, New York, in 1843 as "a glorious document" whose "sentiments . . . fell in burning eloquence" on the hearts of the revolutionary generation.[89]

In his celebrated pamphlet, *Appeal* [. . .] *to the Coloured Citizens of the World*, black abolitionist David Walker challenged Americans to consider the hypocrisy that the Declaration illuminated. "Compare your own language . . . from your Declaration of Independence," he demanded,

> with your cruelties and murders inflicted by your cruel and unmerciful fathers. . . .

> Now, Americans! I ask you candidly, was your sufferings under Great Britain, one hundredth part as cruel and tyrannical as you have rendered ours under you?[90]

It similarly enraged the most famous of American abolitionists, William Lloyd Garrison, that "every Fourth of July, our Declaration of Independence is produced, with a sublime indignation, to set forth the tyranny of the mother country," when side by side Americans practiced "such a glaring contradiction as exists between our creed and practice."[91] Garrison was not sure he could "stand up before a European assembly, and exult that [he was] an American citizen," without "the recollection of [his] country's barbarity and despotism" blistering [his] lips.[92] The nation that had unfurled the Declaration as its banner and proposed to fling it out to the world as an example—"We, the boasted pattern for the world"—had "cut down the banner of freedom," exclaimed a contributor to the *Oberlin Evangelist* four months after Calhoun spoke of the Declaration as dangerous, "and planted in its stead the black flag of slavery!!"[93]

But the attempt to diminish the Declaration and the American Revolution in the interests of slavery met its most famous rhetorical check in the famous 1858 debates between Stephen A. Douglas and Lincoln as both vied for the senior US Senate seat from Illinois. From the opening of the campaign in July 1858 until Election Day in November, Douglas never stopped declaring that Lincoln's opposition to slavery meant that Lincoln wanted to abolish slavery, move the freed slaves into Illinois, and give them equal civil rights with white Illinoisans.

> I ask you, are you in favor of conferring upon the negro the rights and privileges of citizenship? Do you desire to strike out of our state constitution that clause which keeps slaves and free negroes out of the state, and allow the free negroes to flow in, and cover your prairies with black settlements? Do you desire to turn this beautiful state into a free negro colony in order that when Missouri abolishes slavery, she can send one

> hundred thousand emancipated slaves into Illinois to become citizens and voters on an equality with yourselves? If you desire negro citizenship, if you desire to allow them to come into the state and settle with the white man, if you desire them to vote on an equality with yourselves, and to make them eligible to office, to serve on juries, and to judge your rights, then support Mr. Lincoln and the Black Republican party, who are in favor of the citizenship of the negro.[94]

Douglas was, at that moment, performing two tricks in political theory: One was his insistence that any advocacy of equal rights included *all* rights—natural, civil, and social; the other was his equally tenacious insistence that black people were not people in the sense the Declaration intended when it described all men as created equal. Douglas believed that the United States was "made by white men, for the benefit of white men and their posterity forever, and I am in favor of confining citizenship to white men, men of European birth and descent, instead of conferring it upon negroes, Indians and other inferior races."[95]

In reply, Lincoln defended the Declaration's absolutism on equality, which placed him squarely on the side of black humanity. "Let us discard all this quibbling about . . . this race and that race and the other race being inferior, and therefore they must be placed in an inferior position," Lincoln urged at the beginning of the Lincoln–Douglas contest of 1858.[96] But he drew a common 19th-century distinction between the natural rights and civil and social rights to which that humanity was entitled. Natural rights were the inalienable endowment enjoyed by every human being, regardless of race, nationality, or even gender; civil and social rights were bestowed by political communities so that different nations may award different opportunities in different ways to different portions of their societies.

Lincoln was not bold enough in 1858 to insist that the Declaration mandated civil and social rights. "I have no purpose to introduce political and social equality between the white and black races," he answered Douglas. But he did make it clear that African Americans unquestionably enjoyed an equality of *natural* rights that made slavery an impossibility in a free republic. Lincoln held that "there is no reason in the world why the negro is not entitled to all the rights enumerated in the Declaration of Independence—the right of life, liberty and the pursuit of happiness"—and that "he is as much entitled to these as the white man." Determinations about civil and social rights were the privilege of democratic societies, but not natural rights, which were nonnegotiable. "In the right to eat the bread without the leave of anybody else which his own hand earns, he is my equal and the equal of Judge Douglas, and the equal of every other man," Lincoln concluded.[97]

Their Immortal Declaration

It would take a bloody civil war to lay Calhoun's dissent—a dissent from the centrality of the American Revolution and the Declaration of Independence as events of world-historical import—in the dust. That war was led by Lincoln, who protested that its outcome would reestablish the republic on the "proposition" that had been articulated "four score and seven years" before.[98] In that respect, the Civil War was really a war to decide the long-term outcome of the Revolution—whether it was strictly an 18th-century political event or whether it embodied ideas with irresistible and ongoing application.

At its close, Lincoln's secretary of state and onetime rival, William Henry Seward, pleaded for national reconciliation by appealing to the remembrance of the Revolution and its principles. "The people who have so steadily adhered to the true path of democratic progress and civilization . . . through so many difficulties and at such fearful cost in war," he suggested, will now surely have new "inducements and encouragements to persevere" in "the political equality of all men, which the founders, in their immortal declaration, laid down as the true basis of the Union."[99]

But the place of the Revolution in American historical memory was already shifting. By the 1876 centennial exposition in Philadelphia, it was appearing in new garb as the freedom to invent new technology. The Revolution would be celebrated for not only American "victories over enemies, foreign and domestic," but

> victories over climate, earth and water . . . clearing away the forests . . . inventing the locomotive engine, to carry, whither they will, the millions of people of the Old World seeking here free homes; inventing the telegraph, to annihilate time and space . . . the sewing machine, to emancipate women from their life's chief drudgery. . . . We but stand upon the threshold of our greatness.[100]

Only 30 years later, the historian Carl Lotus Becker would formulate his famous progressive objection that the Revolution was as much about who would rule at home as it was about home rule. Becker would be followed in 1913 by Charles A. Beard's even more progressive insistence that the founders were a self-interested elite whose chief aim in the Revolution was cementing their own class power. "Our fundamental law was not the product of an abstraction known as the 'whole people,'" Beard proposed in *An Economic Interpretation of the Constitution of the United States*, "but of a group of economic interests which must have expected beneficial results from its adoption."[101]

Like Calhoun, progressivism erased principle for interest, replacing race with class as the hidden hand in the American founding. Like Calhoun again, progressives produced a worldly wise understanding of the Revolution, and it blends conveniently with a postmodern sensibility that reduces all propositions to matters of mere economic power. Whether this sensibility is anything that the first 100 years of the Revolution and the Declaration would recognize is another question, one that the 250th anniversary of independence cannot avoid pondering.

Notes

1. *The Pennsylvania Evening Post*, "Philadelphia," July 5, 1777.
2. *The Pennsylvania Evening Post*, "Philadelphia."
3. David Sharp, "Tens of Millions Americans Crisscross the Country to Celebrate the Fourth of July," PBS News, July 4, 2024, https://www.pbs.org/newshour/nation/tens-of-millions-americans-crisscross-the-country-to-celebrate-the-fourth-of-july.
4. Stephanie Farr, "Philly's New Independence Holiday Gets to the Heart of America," *The Philadelphia Inquirer*, July 3, 2024, https://www.inquirer.com/columnists/philadelphia-july-4-events-new-red-white-and-blue-to-do-20240703.html.
5. Peter Thompson, "Local Safety, National Violence," *Commonplace* 14, no. 3 (2014), https://commonplace.online/article/local-safety-national-violence/.
6. Michel Foucault, "On the Genealogy of Ethics: An Overview of a Work in Progress," in *The Foucault Reader*, ed. Paul Rabinow (Pantheon Books, 1984), 343.
7. Paul Finkelman, "The First Civil Rights Movement: Black Rights in the Age of the Revolution and Chief Taney's Originalism in *Dred Scott*," *University of Pennsylvania Journal of Constitutional Law* 24, no. 3 (2022): 707, https://scholarship.law.upenn.edu/jcl/vol24/iss3/2/.
8. Quoted in Cushing Strout, *The American Image of the Old World* (Harper & Row, 1963), 67.
9. Abraham Lincoln, "Address to the New Jersey State Senate at Trenton, New Jersey," in *The Collected Works of Abraham Lincoln*, ed. Roy P. Basler, vol. 4, *1860–1861* (Rutgers University Press, 1953), 235–36.
10. Frederick Douglass, *Oration, Delivered in Corinthian Hall, Rochester* (Rochester, NY, 1852), 15.
11. Abraham Lincoln, "To George Robertson," in *The Collected Works of Abraham Lincoln*, vol. 2, *1848–1858*, 317.
12. Sarah Logan Fisher, January 13, 1777, diary entry, in Nicholas B. Wainwright, "'A Diary of Trifling Occurrences': Philadelphia, 1776–1778," *The Pennsylvania Magazine of History and Biography* 82, no. 4 (1958): 422, https://www.jstor.org/stable/20089127.
13. Elizabeth Drinker, July 4, 1777, diary entry, in *The Diary of Elizabeth Drinker: The Life Cycle of an Eighteenth-Century Woman*, ed. Elaine Forman Crane (University of Pennsylvania Press, 2010), 60; and Richard Godbeer, *World of Trouble: A Philadelphia Quaker Family's Journey Through the American Revolution* (Yale University Press, 2019), 137.
14. *Federalist*, no. 1 (Alexander Hamilton), https://founders.archives.gov/documents/Hamilton/01-04-02-0152.
15. David Ramsay, *The History of the American Revolution* (Philadelphia, 1789), 1:27, 347, 350.
16. *Aurora & General Advertiser*, "New York, July 17," July 19, 1792.

17. Pauline Maier, *American Scripture: Making the Declaration of Independence* (Knopf, 1997), 171. Michael Kammen argues to the contrary that Americans in the early republic were too busy to pay attention to their history, and he takes perhaps too seriously the complaints of John Adams that "the history of our Country is getting full of Falshoods and it is high time for some of them to be corrected." Michael Kammen, *Mystic Chords of Memory: The Transformation of Tradition in American Culture* (Knopf, 1991), 49.

18. Thomas A. Chambers, *Memories of War: Visiting Battlegrounds and Bonefields in the Early American Republic* (Cornell University Press, 2012), 84–90.

19. *Aurora & General Advertiser*, "Philadelphia," July 9, 1798. The cornerstone for the Saratoga battlefield monument was not laid until 1877; the monument honoring Nathanael Greene at Guilford Courthouse was not dedicated until 1915.

20. *Philadelphia North American*, "Fourth of July," July 12, 1798.

21. William Swinton, *First Lessons in Our Country's History: Bringing Out Its Salient Points, and Aiming to Combine Simplicity with Sense* (New York, 1872), 87.

22. *The Freeman's Journal, or, the North American Intelligencer*, "New-York, July 11," July 16, 1788; and Adam J. Criblez, *Parading Patriotism: Independence Day Celebrations in the Urban Midwest, 1826–1876* (Northern Illinois University Press, 2013), 13.

23. *New-York Evening Post*, "American Independence," July 21, 1813.

24. *Cleveland Plain Dealer*, "Correspondence of the Plain Dealer," July 9, 1845.

25. Paul Finkelman, "Master John Marshall and the Problem of Slavery," *The University of Chicago Law Review*, August 31, 2020, 6, https://lawreview.uchicago.edu/online-archive/master-john-marshall-and-problem-slavery.

26. David Waldstreicher, "Rites of Rebellion, Rites of Assent: Celebrations, Print Culture, and the Origins of American Nationalism," *The Journal of American History* 82, no. 1 (1995): 3, https://academic.oup.com/jah/article-abstract/82/1/37/737797.

27. Paul Goetsch, "The Fourth of July and Its Role in American Literature," in *The Fourth of July: Political Oratory and Literary Reactions, 1776–1876*, ed. Paul Goetsch and Gerd Hurm (Gunter Narr Verlag, 1992), 46; and Len Travers, "Hurrah for the Fourth: Patriotism, Politics, and Independence Day in Federalist Boston, 1783–1818," *Essex Institute Historical Collections* 125, no. 2 (1989): 134–35, https://babel.hathitrust.org/cgi/pt?id=mdp.39015052932962&seq=139.

28. Edward Everett, "The Seven Years' War the School of the Revolution," in *Orations and Speeches on Various Occasions* (Boston, 1859), 1:377–78.

29. Abraham Lincoln, "Response to a Serenade," in *The Collected Works of Abraham Lincoln*, vol. 6, *1862–1863*, 320.

30. Thomas Paine, *A Letter Addressed to the Abbe Raynal, on the Affairs of North America, in Which the Mistakes in the Abbe's Account of the Revolution of America Are Corrected and Cleared Up* (London, 1817), 37.

31. Francis Wayland, "The Duties of an American Citizen," in *Occasional Discourses, Including Several Never Before Published* (Boston, 1833), 64.

32. David Ramsay, "An Oration on the Advantages of American Independence," in *David Ramsay, 1749–1815: Selections from His Writings*, ed. Robert L. Brunhouse (American Philosophical Society, 1965), 188.

33. James Kirke Paulding, *The Backwoodsman: A Poem* (Philadelphia, 1818), 34.

34. *New-York Evening Post*, "Friday, July 6," July 6, 1804.

35. Charles J. Ingersoll, *A Communication on the Improvement of Government: Read Before the American Philosophical Society, at a Meeting Attended by General Lafayette, October 1st, 1824* (Philadelphia, 1824), 7–8, 10.

36. *Richmond Enquirer*, "The Jubilee of Liberty," July 4, 1826.

37. William H. Crawford, July 4, 1813, in *The Journal of William H. Crawford*, ed. Daniel Chauncey Knowlton (Department of History of Smith College, 1925), 11:19.

38. Paul A. Johnsgard, *Lewis and Clark on the Great Plains: A Natural History* (University of Nebraska Press, 2003), 106.

39. *Cleveland Plain Dealer*, "The Celebration," July 5, 1845.

40. *Illinois State Register*, "Juvenile Celebration," July 4, 1845.

41. *Gazette of the United States*, "The Day," July 4, 1826.

42. Enoch Cobb Wines, *Hints on a System of Popular Education: Addressed to R. S. Field, Esq.* (Philadelphia, 1838), 247–48.

43. John Russell, *A History of the United States of America, from the Period of Discovery to the Present Time: Arranged for the Use of Schools, with Questions for the Examination of Students* (Philadelphia, 1838), 116, 204.

44. Abbé Fauchet, "Extract from the Eulogy on Dr. Franklin, Pronounced by the Abbe Fauchet, in the Name of the Commons of Paris, 1790," in *The Columbian Orator* [. . .], ed. Caleb Bingham, 18th ed. (New York, 1816), 67; and Arthur O'Connor, "Part of Mr. O'Connor's Speech in the Irish House of Commons, in Favor of the Bill for Emancipating the Roman Catholics, 1795," in Bingham, *The Columbian Orator*, 247.

45. Caleb Bingham, *The American Preceptor: Being a New Selection of Lessons for Reading and Speaking* (Boston, 1801), 48–50.

46. Bingham, *The American Preceptor*, 48–50.

47. John Stauffer, *Giants: The Parallel Lives of Frederick Douglass and Abraham Lincoln* (Hachette, 2009).

48. Abraham Lincoln, "Report of Speech at Vandalia, Illinois, 23 September 1856," speech, Vandalia, IL, September 23, 1856, https://papersofabrahamlincoln.org/documents/D200923.

49. Abraham Lincoln, "First Debate with Stephen A. Douglas at Ottawa, Illinois," in *The Collected Works of Abraham Lincoln*, vol. 3, *1858–1860*, 18–19.

50. Abraham Lincoln, "Farewell Address at Springfield, Illinois," in *The Collected Works of Abraham Lincoln*, vol. 4, *1860–1861*, 190; and Lincoln, "Address to the New Jersey State Senate at Trenton, New Jersey," 235–36, 240.

51. Abraham Lincoln, "Speech in Independence Hall, Philadelphia, Pennsylvania," in *The Collected Works of Abraham Lincoln*, vol. 4, *1860–1861*, 240.

52. Jefferson Davis, "Inaugural Address of the President of the Provisional Government," in *Jefferson Davis, Constitutionalist: His Letters, Papers and Speeches*, ed. Dunbar Rowland (Mississippi Department of Archives and History, 1923), 5:50.

53. Emory M. Thomas, "Jefferson Davis and the American Revolutionary Tradition," *Journal of the Illinois State Historical Society* 70, no. 1 (1977): 6–7.

54. *New York Daily Herald*, "The Monster Meeting," April 21, 1861; and John Cochrane, "Speech of Hon. John Cochrane," *New York Daily Herald*, April 21, 1861.

55. *Chicago Tribune*, "The Nation's Crisis," April 15, 1861.

56. *Chicago Tribune*, "All for Our Country," April 16, 1861.

57. Stephen Foster, "I'm Nothing but a Plain Old Soldier," in *Classic Songs*, ed. Matthew Barton (Sterling, 2008), 248.

58. Alexander Wallace Givin, July 21, 1862, diary entry, Union League of Philadelphia Archives.

59. Thomas Jefferson, "Jefferson's 'Original Rough Draught' of the Declaration of Independence," in *The Papers of Thomas Jefferson*, ed. Julian P. Boyd, vol. 1, *1760–1776* (Princeton University Press, 1950), 246–47.

60. Thomas Jefferson, *A Summary View of the Rights of British America* (London, 1774), 28–29.

61. Thomas Jefferson to Lydia Howard Huntley Sigourney, July 18, 1824, Founders Online, https://founders.archives.gov/documents/Jefferson/98-01-02-4419.

62. Jefferson, *A Summary View of the Rights of British America*, 28–29; David Brion Davis, *The Problem of Slavery in the Age of Revolution 1770–1823*, 2nd ed. (Oxford University Press, 1999), 9–10; Thomas Jefferson to John Holmes, April 22, 1820, in *The Portable Thomas Jefferson*, ed. Merrill D. Peterson (Viking, 1975), 568; and Michael Zuckerman, "The Power of Blackness: Thomas Jefferson and the Revolution in St. Domingue," in *Almost Chosen People: Oblique Biographies in the American Grain* (University of California Press, 1993), 214–16.

63. James Madison to Joseph Jones, November 28, 1780, in *The Papers of James Madison*, ed. William T. Hutchinson and William M. E. Rachal, vol. 2, *20 March 1780–23 February 1781* (University of Chicago Press, 1962), 209.

64. James Madison to James Madison Sr., September 8, 1783, in *The Papers of James Madison*, vol. 7, *3 May 1783–29 February 1784*, 304–5.

65. James Madison to Edmund Randolph, July 26, 1785, in *The Papers of James Madison*, vol. 8, *10 March 1784–28 March 1786*, 329. On this incident, see also Jeff Broadwater, *James Madison: A Son of Virginia and a Founder of the Nation* (University of North Carolina Press, 2012), 115.

66. Quoted in Eva Sheppard Wolf, *Race and Liberty in the New Nation: Emancipation in Virginia from the Revolution to Nat Turner's Rebellion* (Louisiana State University Press, 2006), 1. Eva Sheppard Wolf quotes the *Virginia Gazette* in 1782. But the original author of this nettling inquiry seems to have been John Cooper of Gloucester, New Jersey, in *The New-Jersey Gazette* on September 20, 1780. See John Cooper, "To the Publick," *The New-Jersey Gazette*, September 20, 1780, 2, https://www.loc.gov/resource/sn83025471/1780-09-20/ed-1/.

67. *The New-Jersey Gazette*, quoted in Winthrop D. Jordan, *White over Black: American Attitudes Toward the Negro, 1550–1812* (University of North Carolina Press, 1968), 378.

68. *Journal of the House of Representatives of the United States, Being the First Session of the Fifth Congress, Begun and Held at the City of Philadelphia, May 15, 1797, and in the Twenty-First Year of the Independence of the Said States* (Washington, 1826), 3:550.

69. Sean Wilentz, *No Property in Man: Slavery and Antislavery at the Nation's Founding* (Harvard University Press, 2018), 154, 165, 167–69, 176; David Stone and John Quincy Adams, "1804, Tuesday, Jany. 31. Bill Relating to Louisiana," in Everett Somerville Brown, *The Constitutional History of the Louisiana Purchase, 1803–1812* (University of California Press, 1920), 224; and David Stone and John Quincy Adams, "1804, Friday, Feby. 17. Louisiana Bill," in Brown, *The Constitutional History of the Louisiana Purchase, 1803–1812*, 232.

70. Robert Jefferson Breckinridge, "From the Genius of Universal Emancipation," in *The Spirit of Humanity and Essence of Morality: Extracted from the Productions of the Enlightened and Benevolent of Various Ages and Climes* (Albany, NY, 1835), 268.

71. Tim Matthewson, "Jefferson and the Nonrecognition of Haiti," *Proceedings of the American Philosophical Society* 140, no. 1 (1996): 23.

72. Forrest Nabors, *From Oligarchy to Republicanism: The Great Task of Reconstruction* (University of Missouri Press, 2017), 143–44.

73. Cong. Globe, 30th Cong., 1st Sess. 876 (1848).

74. John C. Calhoun, "A Disquisition on Government," in *Union and Liberty: The Political Philosophy of John C. Calhoun*, ed. Ross M. Lence (Liberty Fund, 1992), 42.

75. John C. Calhoun, "Speech on the Reception of Abolition Petitions," in *Union and Liberty*, 473; and Cong. Globe, 24th Cong., 2nd Sess. (1837).

76. John C. Calhoun, "Speech on the Oregon Bill," in *The Papers of John C. Calhoun*, ed. Clyde N. Wilson and Shirley Bright Cook, vol. 25, *1847–1848* (University of South Carolina Press, 1999), 535.

77. Calhoun, "Speech on the Oregon Bill," 535.

78. John C. Calhoun, "Exposition and Protest," in *Union and Liberty*, 357; and C. Bradley Thompson, *America's Revolutionary Mind: A Moral History of the American Revolution and the Declaration That Defined It* (Encounter Books, 2019), 362–73.

79. Calhoun, "Exposition and Protest," in *Union and Liberty*, 333–34; Cong. Globe, 22nd Cong., 2nd Sess. 322–23 (1842); and John C. Calhoun, "Speech: On Mr. Clay's

Resolutions in Relation to the Revenues and Expenditures; Delivered in the Senate, March 16th, 1842," in *The Works of John C. Calhoun*, ed. Richard K. Crallé, vol. 4, *Speeches of John C. Calhoun, Delivered in the House of Representatives, and in the Senate of the United States* (New York, 1854), 134.

80. John C. Calhoun to William Ruffin, October 8, 1835, in *The Papers of John C. Calhoun*, ed. Clyde N. Wilson, vol. 12, *1833–1835*, 564.

81. Drew R. McCoy, *The Last of the Fathers: James Madison & the Republican Legacy* (Cambridge University Press, 1989), 234.

82. Stephen V. Ash, *Middle Tennessee Society Transformed, 1860–1870: War and Peace in the Upper South* (Louisiana State University Press, 1988), 40.

83. Henry St. George Tucker, *Lectures on Constitutional Law: For the Use of the Law Class at the University of Virginia* (Richmond, VA, 1843), 46–47.

84. Tucker, *Lectures on Constitutional Law*, 46–47.

85. Thomas Roderick Dew, "An Address, on the Influence of the Federative Republican System of Government upon Literature and the Development of Character," *Southern Literary Messenger* 2, no. 4 (1836): 277, https://quod.lib.umich.edu/m/moajrnl/acf2679.0002.004/226:2.

86. Alexander H. Stephens, "Cornerstone Address," in *Southern Pamphlets on Secession, November 1860–April 1861*, ed. Jon L. Wakelyn (University of North Carolina Press, 1996), 406–7.

87. Stephens, "Cornerstone Address," in *Southern Pamphlets on Secession, November 1860–April 1861*, 406–7.

88. Angelina E. Grimké, "Appeal to the Christian Women of the South," *The Anti-Slavery Examiner* 1, no. 2 (1836): 16.

89. Henry Highland Garnet, "An Address to the Slaves of the United States of America," in *The Black Abolitionist Papers*, ed. C. Peter Ripley et al., vol. 3, *The United States, 1830–1846* (University of North Carolina Press, 1991), 406.

90. David Walker, *Walker's Appeal, in Four Articles: Together with a Preamble, to the Coloured Citizens of the World* (Boston, 1830), 77.

91. Wendell Phillips Garrison and Francis Jackson Garrison, *William Lloyd Garrison, 1805–1879: The Story of His Life Told by His Children*, vol. 1, *1805–1835* (New York, 1885), 131.

92. Benjamin Lamb-Books, *Angry Abolitionists and the Rhetoric of Slavery: Moral Emotions in Social Movements* (Palgrave Macmillan, 2016), 106.

93. Lemuel Foster, "The Presidential Election: A Momentous Issue," *Oberlin Evangelist* 10, no. 4 (1848): 157.

94. Stephen A. Douglas, "First Debate with Stephen A. Douglas at Ottawa, Illinois," in *The Collected Works of Abraham Lincoln*, 3:9.

95. Douglas, "First Debate with Stephen A. Douglas at Ottawa, Illinois."

96. Lincoln, "Speech at Chicago, Illinois," in *The Collected Works of Abraham Lincoln*, vol. 2, *1848–1858*, 501.

97. Abraham Lincoln, "Sixth Debate with Stephen A. Douglas, at Quincy, Illinois," in *The Collected Works of Abraham Lincoln*, vol. 3, *1858–1860*, 248–49.

98. Abraham Lincoln, "The Gettysburg Address," speech, Gettysburg, PA, November 19, 1863, https://www.abrahamlincolnonline.org/lincoln/speeches/gettysburg.htm.

99. William Henry Seward, "The President and His Cabinet," in *The Works of William H. Seward*, ed. George E. Baker, vol. 5, *The Diplomatic History of the War for the Union, Etc.* (Boston, 1884), 522.

100. *Philadelphia Inquirer*, "One Hundred Years Ago," July 4, 1876.

101. Charles A. Beard, *An Economic Interpretation of the Constitution of the United States* (Macmillan, 1913), 17; and Alan Gibson, *Understanding the Founding: The Crucial Questions*, 2nd ed. (University Press of Kansas, 2010), 21–31. As Finkelman has observed, Beard almost never talked about slavery and showed little interest in abolition or civil rights.

4

Teaching the Revolution

RITA KOGANZON

To ask how American schools have taught the American Revolution is to pose a question of epic proportions. In almost no national undertaking is the "administrative decentralization" that Alexis de Tocqueville praised in the United States more obvious than in education.

Even if we sought only what *public* schools taught, we are faced with the reality that the United States is a nation of almost 100,000 public elementary and secondary schools and over 13,000 districts in 50 states, with each jurisdiction exerting varying degrees of control over each school's curriculum.[1] Add to that 30,000 private schools and an uncertain number of alternative configurations like homeschools, virtual schools, and co-ops educating up to two million additional students, and the hope of determining with any certainty what American schools teach or what students learn rapidly dims.[2]

Indeed, an essential part of what schools teach students about our regime is encoded in this decentralized structure itself: federalism, free association, and, most importantly, self-government. Salutary as these structures are, however, they don't make the task of surveying the changing place of the founding in American education easier.

One imperfect way around this obstacle is to examine the changing character of American schoolbooks. From *The Columbian Orator*, which inspired Frederick Douglass's efforts to realize the promises of the Declaration of Independence, to William McGuffey's Eclectic Readers, which shaped millions of children in 19th-century America, to Harold Rugg's progressive and ultimately divisive Man and His Changing Society series, to more recent works like *The 1619 Project*, an essay anthology developed by *The New York Times*, American history textbooks have themselves become part of our history. The shifts in their depictions of the American founding point to deeper shifts in national perceptions of the place and significance of the Revolution in American life.

On their own, of course, American textbooks cannot possibly encompass the whole endeavor of American civic or historical education. For one thing, textbooks are inert. They tell us only what their authors wrote in them but nothing about how teachers taught them or how pupils understood them, if they understood them at all. Undoubtedly, my classmates were not the first for whom the primary purpose of their history textbooks was to supply them with rolling paper. What goes unlearned from textbooks, moreover, does not simply remain unknown, because unlike other subjects learned exclusively by academic study, by far the most potent source of knowledge about our political regime comes from living in it.

Worse still, to the extent that textbooks have been significant sources of civic education, they have hardly spoken in one voice. While the market for textbooks was much smaller in the 19th century, such that a single series like McGuffey's readers could really be said to dominate it absolutely, by the 20th century hundreds of titles competed for school use at any given moment. But even as early as 1797, Caleb Bingham, author of *The Columbian Orator*, could open his offering with "Notwithstanding the multiplicity of School-Books now in use, . . ."[3] First sectional tension, then ideological difference resulted in the publication of books designed explicitly to promote alternative historical narratives.

Without downplaying these significant shortcomings of using textbooks as metonyms for American education, the changes in their presentation of the Revolution and the founding period nonetheless illuminate something of how Americans' sense of their nation has changed. Given the market-driven nature of textbooks, successful entrants always had to reflect not just what authors believed but to some degree also what authors thought teachers, school boards, and parents wanted children to learn. In the mid-20th century, the development of formal district- and state-based adoption processes added another layer of popular input into textbook content.[4] And while the textbook market is fractured, some titles have always predominated and achieved widespread national use and approbation or—equally significantly—national controversy.

This chapter focuses on a small selection of such books, which have transcended regional and sectional boundaries and encroached on the national consciousness. Of course, there have been many others. To examine only a handful of titles across more than 200 years is not to offer a full picture of American schoolbooks by any means, but for that end, other studies are available to fill the gaps.[5] What we do find when we examine this sampling of textbooks is a distinctive pattern of change in their depiction of the founding.

Through the end of the 19th century, before the development of a comprehensive system of public schooling, American schoolbooks like Bingham's *The Columbian Orator* and McGuffey's Eclectic Readers conscripted history and biography into the service of personal moral formation for their readers. Historical figures, particularly George Washington and a handful of other heroes of the American Revolution, were described not only in terms of their roles in political events but as exemplary individuals in the round, whose virtues were demonstrated by their public and private speeches. These speeches were to be objects of imitation for pupils, who would learn to read and speak by emulating the great rhetoricians of the past and, in the process, imbibe the virtues that their speeches extolled.

But by the turn of the century, American textbooks took on a more detached and scientific character, focused on understanding the country and its founding in the context of impersonal political and economic systems and processes, such as class conflict, industrialization, and democratization. Twentieth-century textbooks deployed history not as a goad to character formation but as one of several social sciences whose mastery would develop skills of social and economic "problem-solving." This shift also entailed a reversal in the books' approach toward the Revolution, which went from a triumph to, at best, a salutary but fumbling step toward gradual progress that would only reach its full potential centuries later. By the 21st century, these trends had come almost full circle, with texts like *The 1619 Project* that rejected the founders outright and raised protest and resistance against government, rather than personal virtue or social reform, to the highest form of citizenship.

Tracing these shifts matters for understanding the cultural legacy of the American Revolution. For more than 200 years, students have been taught that 1776 bequeathed either exemplars to emulate, systems to manage, or structures to resist. Each stance disposes citizens differently toward the founders, political agency, and self-government. And these changes have not gone uncontested. Since the beginning of the 20th century, textbooks have been subject to recurring challenge and revision, particularly regarding their depictions of the Revolution. These "history wars" have also reflected latent American uncertainty and conflict about the meaning of the Revolution that we want to transmit to future generations.

The Revolution as Rhetorical and Personal Formation

Although probably not the bestselling school reader of the early republic, Bingham's *The Columbian Orator* was a formidable contender, selling at least 200,000 copies and going through more than a dozen editions during its publication run between 1797 and 1820.[6] A compilation of speeches and dialogues selected to "cultivate the art of oratory," the text made a lifelong impression on 19th-century public intellectuals such as Ralph Waldo Emerson, Harriet Beecher Stowe, Horace Greeley, and, most famously, Frederick Douglass. Douglass first encountered *The Columbian Orator* while still enslaved in Baltimore and credited its antislavery selections with giving "tongue to interesting thoughts of my own soul, which had frequently flashed through my mind, and died away for want of utterance. . . . What I got . . . was . . . a powerful vindication of human rights."[7]

The Columbian Orator, along with its companion volume for younger students, *The American Preceptor*, taught by the example of its sources rather than direct instruction from Bingham. In its earliest editions, it contained about a dozen American selections out of about 80 speeches and dialogues from Rome, France, Britain, and Bingham's own imagination. The dialogues and exhortations composed by Bingham typically encouraged filial obedience, piety, industry, and other standard Christian and republican virtues. But they were not all stuffy or tiresome. For example, a dispute in Hades between the ghosts of an English gentleman and a Mohawk Indian over whose murderous customs were more honorable—dueling or scalping—concludes with the realization that the dissipated Englishman is no less "savage" than the Indian, and less forgivably so, given his purportedly civilized upbringing.[8]

Politically, Bingham's selections promoted expanded schooling and religious toleration and opposed slavery. He took for granted the righteousness of the American Revolution and the cause of liberty, including in his book numerous pro-American English works like William Pitt's and Charles James Fox's parliamentary speeches against British colonial policy in the 1760s and 1770s, as well as encomiums on the French Revolution after the Terror.[9] By the end of its run, the American share of *The Columbian Orator* had nearly doubled, with nearly all the new additions coming from now-obscure New England politicians of the 1790s.[10] But Bingham's American guiding lights remained Washington and Benjamin Franklin, excerpts from and about whom dot every edition of the *Orator* and the *Preceptor*.

By the 1830s, Bingham's books had gone out of print, and a newcomer that would leave an indelible mark on American education for almost a century appeared on the horizon: McGuffey's Eclectic Readers. The readers, which were ultimately graded into six levels that ranged from a basic monosyllabic primer to a serious rhetoric text, were initially published in 1836, with the last two readers written primarily by McGuffey's younger brother. However skeptical we might be of textbooks' formative significance, it would be difficult to overstate these unassuming editions' foundational influence on American education.

Their publication corresponded with the creation and diffusion of the common school movement across the country, particularly into the South and West. For children who did not attend these schools, McGuffey's readers alone often formed the basis of such education as they managed. They were the source of still-ubiquitous American nursery rhymes and children's songs like "Mary Had a Little Lamb" and "Twinkle, Twinkle, Little Star." One historian observed that by 1850, when the American population stood at 16 million, seven million of the readers had been sold. By 1890, 100 million more had been published.[11]

If there was one overarching teaching of the readers, it was personal virtue—or, as some have more cynically construed it, the suggestion that "virtue pays." Most of McGuffey's stories feature children being rewarded, and sometimes literally paid, for their sacrifices.[12] For example, a girl who gives up her piece of cake to a sick and hungry dog and his owner gets another cake and the satisfaction of contributing to the ailing duo's recuperation.[13]

But while McGuffey extols bourgeois virtues like industriousness and thrift, he does not privilege them over piety, patriotism, and being loved by one's friends and family. A boy who resists the urge to eat the strawberries he picked so he can bring them to his sick mother instead is rewarded with only her gratitude and blessing, which McGuffey assures his reader brings the boy twice the happiness that eating the strawberries himself would have accorded.[14]

Wealth is a less reliable reward for virtue than happiness, as another "good boy whose parents are poor" reflects after a long day of helping his family:

> I have often been told, and I have read, that it is God who makes some poor, and others rich;—that the rich have many troubles which we know nothing of, and that the poor, if they are but good, may be very happy: indeed, I think that when I am good, nobody can be happier than I am.[15]

A less cynical and more accurate scholarly account of McGuffey's efforts is that "the readers made two essential points: people must learn to resist immediate impulse to have the discipline to pursue higher things, and they must care about those around them."[16]

The Revolution and the founders are also woven quite seamlessly into the readers' overarching teaching. As the historian Johann N. Neem notes, "At the heart of *McGuffey's Readers* was a reminder that individual success was linked to the health and well-being of one's community. Various selections invoked the beauty of America's landscape and its ideals of liberty to foster in students a love of their country."[17]

They also invoked and lionized the heroes of the American founding. Washington, the Marquis de Lafayette, and Christopher Columbus appear interspersed in the early readers as characters exemplifying the same virtues that suffuse McGuffey's other stories and excerpts.

Washington is portrayed as a child himself, learning lessons in piety and honesty from his father. *The Eclectic Second Reader*, for example, includes Mason Weems's apocryphal story of Washington chopping down the cherry tree as a lesson in honesty and a story about Washington's father planting cabbages spelling his name to teach the young George about the providential design of nature.[18] Lafayette is praised for his selflessness and modesty in "cheerfully [spending] his time and fortune" to secure "our liberties."[19] This is, of course, a simplification of his motives, but in a manner that allows children to imitate him.

Starting with the *Eclectic Fourth Reader*, McGuffey, in the tradition of *The Columbian Orator*, relied more on excerpts of speeches, essays, and poems than on his or his brother's original writings, and his selections included more overtly political texts. The *Fourth Reader* includes excerpts from Thomas Paine's writings, Daniel Webster's speech on Washington's birthday, and Thomas Jefferson's reconstruction of the Mingo leader Chief Logan's lament over the murder of his family by white settlers, which had also appeared in Bingham's *Orator*. The fifth and sixth readers, first published in the 1850s, similarly duplicate some of Bingham's selections, including speeches by the British Prime Ministers William Pitt and Robert Walpole. They also include Patrick Henry's 1775 "give me liberty or give me death" speech at the Virginia Convention and the 1830

Senate tariff debates between Webster and Robert Hayne, along with other Webster speeches and writings by Franklin.

If one were to attempt to classify these early textbook efforts politically, it might be fair to understand them as a formation in civic republican ideals, with a decidedly Whig flavor by the 1850s. But rather than merely conveying historical information, their primary purpose was character formation. While they included sketches of chronology and significant historical events, they more commonly focused on introducing famous and noble characters, including the Founding Fathers, as heroes for pupils' emulation. Students using Bingham's and McGuffey's readers should not just learn about Washington but should strive to *be* him. For younger pupils, this emulation was to take the form of imitating great men's conduct and virtues, and for this purpose, great men were often shrunk to a more palatable scale, on which they could appear as merely good men, not unlike the better characters a child might meet around town. Hence McGuffey's depiction of Washington as a very conscientious and well-behaved boy.

For older students, elocution was the key to living up to these heroic models. *The Columbian Orator* was forthrightly designed for that purpose, but the Eclectic Readers, despite the contemporary connotations of the term, were also designed to be read *aloud*. Each one came with a set of "suggestions to teachers" for its use and pedagogical tips for improving recitations, which made no functional distinction between learning to read and learning to speak properly.[20] Reading and elocution were not merely to be a mechanical practice, however:

> This book is designed for other purposes than merely to teach the pupil to read. The selections have been made with a constant reference to the improvement of the *mind* as well as to the cultivation of the voice. Many of the lessons require thought, in order to be appreciated, and before they can be comprehended. Some of these require an extensive range of reading and deep reflection, to enable the reader fully to understand

> the allusions, to enter into the spirit, and to realize the excellence of the extracts.[21]

Recitation and comprehension could be distinguished, but they remained connected in practice, with skill at the latter being required to achieve the former most effectively—"to enter into the spirit" of the selection. Douglass's account of the effect of *The Columbian Orator*'s selections on him, that "they gave tongue to interesting thoughts of [his] own soul," reflects this convergence of reading, speaking, and being.[22] Through reading, students could come to a rational account of virtue, but through speech, they would reveal it in their own characters, so the two were yoked and developed in tandem by the extracts and stories of early American textbooks.

Bingham's *The Columbian Orator* and McGuffey's Eclectic Readers presented the American Revolution and its heroes as personalized models of character for each student to emulate through conduct and especially through speech. That this approach, and even just basic training in elocution, is entirely foreign to American education today is not surprising, however, given subsequent developments. A radically different approach and set of assumptions about the purposes of instruction in the American founding followed McGuffey after the final editions of his readers were published, in 1920, almost 50 years after his death.

The Revolution as Social and Economic Problem

At the turn of the 20th century, the country schoolhouse was fading into obsolescence, and the administrative school district, with graded classrooms, set textbooks, normal school–trained instructors, and a hierarchical organizational structure, was rapidly becoming the norm. American schools became the American school system. Urban reformers who aspired to build what the historian David B. Tyack has called "the one best system" of centralized and uniform national schooling never fully achieved their goals, but they managed to impose a good deal of homogeneity onto previously quite heterogeneous local institutions.[23]

In this context, textbooks began to generate national controversy for the first time. Such "history wars" would become recurring events in American education after the Progressive Era, and it was precisely depictions of the American Revolution and the founding that would frequently become the sore point in the controversy. However enthusiastic Americans were for change and progress, it seems there were some idols they hesitated to topple. Moreover, the constellations of interest groups that converged to push back against insufficiently appreciative depictions of the Revolution were broader than we might expect.

The first such war was set off when the arguments of progressive historians like Carl Lotus Becker and Charles A. Beard that the Revolution was fought to protect the economic interests of colonial elites began appearing in school textbooks. Perhaps predictably, patriotic groups like the American Legion, Veterans of Foreign Wars, and Daughters of the American Revolution opposed progressives' depreciation of the founders.

But more surprisingly, so did African Americans and whites who did not descend from British Protestants, who saw in the deflation of the Revolution by progressive thinking a threat to their own quests for representation in the American pantheon.[24] If men like Washington and Jefferson were downgraded to greedy landowners and speculators, what stature could would-be heroes like Casimir Pulaski or Crispus Attucks ever hope to attain? The historian Jonathan Zimmerman argues, "Under this syllogism, any censure of the Founding Fathers weakened the Revolution; weakening the Revolution elevated England; and elevating the English belittled America's other ethnicities."[25]

Ethnic and religious organizations like the Knights of Columbus joined with the Veterans of Foreign Wars and American Legion in opposing the insertion of "the New History" into K–12 education. As Zimmerman notes, "Ironically, ethnic groups often embraced so-called Progressive interpretations of the Civil War, industrialization, and the Progressive era itself. But they refused to apply this socioeconomic analysis to the Revolution, insisting that America's conception and birth remain immaculate."[26] This strange-bedfellows coalition of immigrant groups and patriotic societies lobbied for state bills outlawing any school textbook that "defames our nation's founders," as one Wisconsin law from 1923 put it.[27]

Reverence for the founders consequently held out against the broader shifts in history education even as other erstwhile figures of admiration came under suspicion. But by the 1930s, they too were subject to social and economic analysis. Rugg's *Man and His Changing Society* was a consummate expression of Progressive Era and early New Deal liberal thought, cheering on reforms that diminished the influence of "plutocrats" and corporations and expanded the purview of the central government as democratic victories for the common people. These textbooks were used in over 5,000 school districts at their peak. Zimmerman estimates that they were the most popular social studies textbooks in the country during this period.[28]

Man and His Changing Society began as a series of pamphlets in the 1920s, which Rugg edited into a six-volume textbook series beginning in 1929. Rugg understood his textbooks as a "unified course in the social studies," synthesizing "history, geography, and civics" for the purpose of training "citizens of the world" by "introducing the economic, political, and social problems of American culture."[29] History was a series of "problems of living" amenable to technical solutions, which could be discerned when all the "facts" were clear.[30] The term "problem" appears constantly, at least 400 times across the series, with the fifth volume devoted entirely to an exposition of American problems. Of equal importance is Rugg's insistence that "we live in a new civilization"—another phrase that is repeated dozens of times across the series.[31] As Rugg put it in his prefatory note "to those who use these books,"

> In this book we are trying to help you to understand the world we live in today, and how that world became what it is. It is not only possible for you to understand many of the difficult problems of our new civilization; it is possible also for you to help in solving them. To do so, you should learn some of the

> important facts about the modern world. You should then form your opinion according to the facts you have learned. . . . Try, therefore, to keep an open mind about every problem that you study.[32]

Rugg intended the books for the middle grades, an older audience than McGuffey targeted with his early readers, but the same one targeted by the fourth and later readers. Yet the difference between his approach to history education and McGuffey's, which was still being assigned when Rugg's series was published, could not be starker.

At the outset, Rugg's priorities are an almost perfect inversion of McGuffey's and Bingham's. Political history does not even appear on Rugg's horizon until the fourth volume, *A History of American Government and Culture*. Before that, students learn about what Rugg terms "American Civilization," consisting of the economic and scientific developments that constitute the present "standard of living," which is Rugg's primary definition of a civilization. The second volume extends this "civilizational" examination to Europe, Russia, China, and Japan, focusing on the factors that facilitated (or obstructed) industrialization in each place. The third volume considers American history only in its "economic and social" aspects, which amounts to a chronology of American standards of living in different times and places—in colonial towns, on the frontier, on Southern plantations, in Western mines, and so on.

Instead of individual characters, Rugg presents readers with elaborate and impersonal structures and systems. We learn about how power is generated, trade conducted, and distances traversed. To the extent that commendable (if not quite heroic) individuals do appear, they take the form of inventors like Samuel Morse and Alexander Graham Bell, whose biographies Rugg sketches in a few sentences but who have no particular virtues of character except, implicitly, persistence in the face of skepticism of their inventions.[33] One supposes them worthy of emulation since they advanced our standard of living, but there is little hint from Rugg about how one might go about such emulation. He presents invention itself as largely a matter of luck rather than any concerted plan. The individual agency that animates the characters in 19th-century textbooks is absent here.

When we finally reach the study of American political history, it is framed as a "march toward democracy," a "three-century-long struggle to bring about . . . 'Government of the people, by the people, for the people.'"[34] While optimistic in some ways, the progressives' approach naturally renders America's beginning as a series of undemocratic errors to be corrected rather than achievements meriting celebration. While our founding held some promising seeds for the future, our greatest national achievements—universal suffrage and a strong central government involved in improving the material life and health of all people through planning—are necessarily very recent developments.

In *Man and His Changing Society*, the Revolution takes on precisely this double character as the act of selfish "business leaders" who above all looked out for their class interests but also (often opportunistically) expressed higher principles that would ultimately result in the overthrow of their own "aristocratic" privileges. Rugg describes the colonial era as beset with conflict between the "ruling classes," composed of wealthy landowners who "had a real contempt for the rank and file of the people," and the "mass of the people," who were constantly struggling for (and occasionally, as in the case of Bacon's Rebellion, winning) a more democratic society.[35] The Revolution came about because of an analogous class antagonism between the colonies and Britain, where "a small group of wealthy landowners and merchants were gaining control of Parliament."[36] This thrust all the colonists together into the position of "the people" vis-à-vis Britain, a division that trumped their prior intra-colonial class conflicts.

Individuals do appear in Rugg's economy-centric narrative of the Revolution, but they are not characters so much as historical handymen who drop in from nowhere to perform some essential political task. For example, James Otis was a "young colonial lawyer" who gave a rousing defense of the Boston merchants, Samuel Adams was a "busy man" who orchestrated the Committees of Correspondence, and Patrick Henry gave a "thrilling" speech at the Virginia Convention, a few lines of which are excerpted.[37] These tasks accomplished, each departs the stage, never to be heard from again. Were these good men or mediocrities? It is not Rugg's task to render such judgments.

The only exception to this value-free submersion of individual character and agency is Washington. While Washington isn't quite above the class struggle that animates all Rugg's history, he is the only founder about whom Rugg offers an explicitly positive assessment: "Were his wealth and experience the only reasons for the confidence people gave him? No, indeed. He had other qualities for which even his enemies honored him—the qualities of a great and generous character."[38] However, Rugg does not elaborate what such qualities might be. Even a great and generous character is just a fact, not intended for imitation or emulation by the reader.

Rugg's more characteristic form of praise, however, is far more grudging. The delegates to the 1787 Constitutional Convention, for example, were "intelligent, even brilliant Americans," but unfortunately from the "well-to-do and prosperous classes" and "exceedingly conservative."[39] The result was a constitution whereby "the merchants, the landowners, the manufacturers, the shippers, and the bankers were given what they wanted, namely, a government which would stabilize money and trade, keep order within the country, and defend the nation against foreign enemies."[40] While commendable in some ways, this Constitution was ultimately incompatible with the changing needs of the people. "The American Constitution was planned to provide for a stable, conservative, slowly changing government. Practically every provision prevented rapid change," Rugg argues.[41] But "even before 1900, a totally new civilization had been produced. . . . In this new civilization change is the most important characteristic." Rugg invites readers to ask, "Did the Constitution of the United States and the business of government change to keep pace with the new manner of living?"[42] The answer is of course a foregone conclusion.

Despite its enormous popularity in the 1930s, by the early 1940s Rugg's opposition to free enterprise itself encountered opposition, and his books inspired another "history war" advanced by a coalition of business and political groups spearheaded by the American Legion.[43] After several years of unrelenting criticism and removal efforts, the series fell out of favor by the mid-1940s.[44] During the Cold War, Rugg's overt anti-capitalism and praise of the Soviet Union largely disappeared from mainstream textbooks, and the Revolution once again excited praise. Consensus history texts like Thomas Bailey's 1956 *American Pageant* appended many flattering adjectives to revolutionary leaders ("George Washington was a giant among men; Benjamin Franklin was a master among diplomats," reads one characteristic line[45]), but there was not much greater depth to their characterizations than Rugg had given.

Rugg's ideological orientation cost him his battle in the history wars, but his broader skepticism won out. Rugg's underlying progressive vision lived on in the "unfinished nation" paradigm that would come to dominate 20th-century textbooks long after his own had been dethroned.[46] On this view, the United States was founded in the pursuit of noble principles but could only gradually realize these principles through group conflict and struggle over time and even today falls short of its visionary aims.[47] The "unfinished nation" paradigm has the advantage of allowing textbook writers to account for recent or current injustices with optimism: Things may not be perfect yet, but they are ever on a trajectory toward improvement. The cost of this framework, however, is that it always entails a faintly patronizing attitude toward a benighted past, limiting even writers who might wish to depict the Revolution and its leaders as exemplary. In a narrative in which the arc of history bends toward justice, the arc itself becomes the main character in history rather than any individuals who shaped events.

The Return of Personalism?

Although McGuffey's readers have maintained something of a cult following among homeschoolers, it is difficult to imagine a wholesale return to Bingham and McGuffey's approach to American history in schools today.

Not only would their moral elevation of the founders and their vision of character formation be unappetizing to a large swath of Americans, but also much more basically, their de-emphasis of chronology and narrative history in favor of biographical sketch and rhetorical extract is incongruent with modern standards for history instruction. For all his ideological baggage, Rugg wrote a thorough and at times even lively narrative chronology of American history. Even conservative critics today would have to laud the comprehensiveness of Rugg's account compared with the truncated and infographic-infested options that dominate the modern textbook market.[48] Chronological narrative is now indisputably necessary in history education.

Nonetheless, perhaps the highly moralistic and personalized approach of 19th-century education *has* resurfaced in the present another way. History texts like *The 1619 Project*, the most recent combatant in our recurring history wars, focus a good deal on individuals and grant them substantial agency, delving extensively into the lives and motives of revolutionary figures like Jefferson.[49] But while McGuffey sought to elevate exemplary historic individuals for pupils to imitate, *The 1619 Project* inverts this aim. For example, it dilates on Jefferson only to demonstrate that he was a hypocrite and a rapist, a villain rather than a hero.

The journalist Nikole Hannah-Jones, who created the 1619 Project and wrote its lead essay, is entirely frank about her intention to achieve precisely this inversion in the culture at large:

> Origin stories function, to a degree, as myths designed to create a shared sense of history and purpose. . . . The origin story of the United States . . . portrays an intrepid, freedom-loving people. . . . This mythology has positioned almost exclusively white Americans as the architects and champions of democracy. . . .
>
> But as this book has shown, a truer origin story requires us to place Black Americans prominently in the role of democracy's defenders and perfecters.[50]

The necessity of downgrading the founders is clear from this, though like so many critical historians of the 20th century, Hannah-Jones cannot entirely deny the revolutionary cause itself, since the pursuit of liberty and equality remains her lodestar. What is odd is what follows on this downgrading of the men who made the Revolution. One might assume that the project of "placing Black Americans prominently in the role of democracy's defenders" would mean replacing one set of (white) national heroes with a more genuinely heroic (black) set and that it might even do so in ways quite reminiscent of McGuffey and Bingham, with their emphasis on the connection between character and speech. Hannah-Jones does go on to offer a list of black protectors of democracy, several of whom wrote and spoke in ways that would make them ideal candidates for inclusion in a 19th-century type of textbook, such as David Walker, Ida B. Wells, and Fannie Lou Hamer. But beyond appending them to this list of potential counter-heroes, *The 1619 Project* hardly mentions them.

The 1619 Project thus obliquely recovers McGuffeyan personalism and concern with individual character, but only for negative ends—to tear down one pantheon of (already quite battered!) heroes, without replacing it with others. Hannah-Jones remains, in this respect, a direct descendant of Rugg and the progressive approach to history, only without the latter's optimism. *The 1619 Project* presents history as governed by impersonal structures and systems. Individual agency, even when exercised by potentially heroic and brilliant individuals like Walker and Wells, is ultimately ineffective against "the racist systems that have undergirded our society for four hundred years."[51]

In Hannah-Jones's telling, while black agency suffers a grim prognosis, the casual choices of long-dead whites like Jefferson and Washington reverberate in our lives to this day. This is in effect the most perverse kind of personalism, in which only villains have agency and everyone else is ground down beneath the behemoth structures and systems that move political events. So unpopular was this framing that five states prohibited *The 1619 Project* in K–12 schools explicitly, and at least 13 others have at least discouraged its use through "divisive concepts" legislation.[52]

Varieties of Oversimplification

It is easy today to deride the moralism and naivete of textbooks like *The Columbian Orator* and the Eclectic Readers. But read in light of what followed the 19th-century paradigm, it appears no less naive and simplistic than its successors. For all that we may charge Bingham and McGuffey with romanticizing the founders, flattening their complexities, or elevating flawed men to undeserved heights, the textbook writers who followed them have done just the same for their preferred protagonists.

Rugg's class-based analysis, despite its patina of sophistication and appeal to expertise ("The course is based upon an elaborate program of research," he boasts in each volume's introduction[53]), is no less reductive. For Rugg, all events arise from class conflict between two clearly delineated groups—the people and the ruling class. The people are never wrong; the ruling class usually is. Rugg's goal is not to teach his readers anything so naive as how to be happy but rather how to solve social problems, and the qualities necessary for that are technical knowledge and an appropriately charitable view of the beneficiaries of one's solutions—the people. Yet for all his solicitousness for the people, Rugg was remarkably shortsighted about the possibility that the social planners running the government would form a new ruling class whose technocratic training would render them contemptuous (to borrow his term) of the very people they had been trained to serve.

Modern texts like *The 1619 Project* and its predecessor, Howard Zinn's *A People's History of the United States*—a popular high school–level American history supplemental synthesis since the 1990s—suffer from similarly destructive simplifications, despite all their pages of scholarly citations. In these books also, the country is divisible into two classes: the ruling class and its victims.

Whereas Rugg concedes that the ruling class can occasionally act in the public interest when that interest is aligned with its self-interest, Hannah-Jones and Zinn depict those in power entirely as predatory villains. To be in power, to govern, is a fundamentally unethical activity, since in their telling no one in American history has governed without oppressing. The only ethically acceptable alternative, and what they hope to cultivate in their readers by depicting the incessant villainy of the powerful, is protest and resistance against power. As a moral teaching, this is just as naive as Rugg's exhortation to technocracy for the sake of democracy. When protest and resistance are the highest forms of citizenship, the skills and responsibilities of statesmanship are devalued, leaving only instability and incompetence in office.[54]

The increasingly utopian hopes that Americans have poured into schooling since the 1830s incline us to want to counter pedagogical naivete with greater sophistication. If Rugg's class binary is too reductive, the solution must be a more nuanced approach to class conflict. Or if Hannah-Jones's racial inversion of the American story is too simplistic, the solution must be greater complexity and ambiguity in our telling of the history of American race relations. But reduction and simplification—even to a degree that appears ridiculous to educated adults—is unavoidable in the teaching of history, which is always ultimately the task of instructing children with, on average, no great enthusiasm for the subject. The only question is who and what will be simplified and reduced. Heroes? Antiheroes? Impersonal forces?

What has remained notably consistent across American textbooks from the founding to the present is a reverence for the American Revolution that even those most intent on deromanticizing America haven't been able to slough off. Even the project of impugning American hypocrisy rests on respect for the promises of the Declaration of Independence, the standard that successive generations can be accused of forsaking. What has changed is the gradual depreciation and demonization of the individuals who signed the Declaration and made the Revolution. But even if we endorse this depreciation, without individuals or much concrete context at all the Revolution becomes an incomprehensible, disembodied abstraction—two lines about self-evident truths plucked from an old parchment that constitute an ideal from an otherwise benighted past that we have still failed to achieve in the present but that somehow ought to animate our future. Who can be surprised if students lose patience with such a convoluted vision?

While it's unlikely and probably undesirable for our textbooks to revert wholesale to the 19th-century paradigm, the history wars of the 20th and 21st centuries have demonstrated that we haven't come up with any stable replacement for it either. The progressive paradigm gained a foothold that subsequently slipped away, and the structural racism paradigm, while initially praised by elite tastemakers, was almost immediately bushwhacked by half the country's state legislatures. What remains is the rudderless liberalism of the "unfinished nation," whose completion is anyone's guess. If national eighth-grade test scores in history and civics and the number of students pursuing history and even political science at the university level indicate anything about the effectiveness of such education, we have some reason to suspect it is going nowhere.[55]

We have little to lose by reconsidering the role of character formation through elocution in elementary education. We would not need to abandon the narrative chronology we have come to view as essential to understanding history to combine it with increased attention to historical biography and rhetoric, the former having been diminished in curricula and the latter almost entirely abandoned (except extracurricular high school debate) despite its continuing centrality to our political life. A return to rhetoric today would almost certainly take its sources from a broader canon of speeches and texts than McGuffey's selections. The subsequent two centuries' worth of material from which to train students in recitation and debate offers a great variety to satisfy a polarized country. For both academic and civic ends, however, it may be salutary for students to try once again to "enter into the spirit" of the American founding.

Notes

1. Maya Riser-Kositsky, "Education Statistics: Facts About American Schools," *Education Week*, August 6, 2025, https://www.edweek.org/leadership/education-statistics-facts-about-american-schools/2019/01.

2. Peter Jamison et al., "Home Schooling's Rise from Fringe to Fastest-Growing Form of Education," *The Washington Post*, October 31, 2025, https://www.washingtonpost.com/education/interactive/2023/homeschooling-growth-data-by-district/.

3. Caleb Bingham, *The Columbian Orator* [. . .] (Boston, 1797).

4. State-based adoption processes have also distorted popular influence by incentivizing publishers to focus on the preferences of the most populous (and so most lucrative) states: California, Texas, Florida, and New York. Even so, these states represent quite different constituencies regionally, demographically, and ideologically, so their dominance still permits a decent diversity of options.

5. For a synoptic study of 19th-century textbooks, see Ruth Miller Elson, *Guardians of Tradition: American Schoolbooks of the Nineteenth Century* (University of Nebraska Press, 1964). On curricular reform and textbooks in the first half of the 20th century, see Herbert M. Kliebard, *The Struggle for the American Curriculum, 1893–1958*, 3rd ed. (Routledge, 2004). On 20th-century conflicts over history textbooks, see Jonathan Zimmerman, *Whose America? Culture Wars in the Public . . . Schools*, 2nd ed. (University of Chicago Press, 2022).

6. *The Columbian Orator*'s primary competitor was Lindley Murray's *The English Reader*, which sold between one and two million copies in the early 19th century. Granville Ganter, "The Active Virtue of *The Columbian Orator*," *The New England Quarterly* 70, no. 3 (1997): 463, https://www.jstor.org/stable/366763.

7. Frederick Douglass, *Narrative of the Life of Frederick Douglass, an American Slave* (Boston, 1845), 39–40.

8. Bingham, *The Columbian Orator*, 53–54.

9. Pitt's and Fox's pro-American speeches are at Bingham, *The Columbian Orator*, 58–60, 156–58, 172–75, 184–85. "Address of Mr. Adet, French Ambassador, on Presenting the Colors of France to the United States, 1796" and Washington's response are at Bingham, *The Columbian Orator*, 85–88. Bingham also includes several speeches of Napoleon's from this period.

10. The 1819 edition, for example, features the poet David Everett and speeches by John Lothrop and John Phillips, father of the more famous orator Wendell Phillips.

11. D. A. Saunders, "Social Ideas in McGuffey Readers," *The Public Opinion Quarterly* 5, no. 4 (1941): 580, https://www.jstor.org/stable/2744701.

12. Saunders, "Social Ideas in McGuffey Readers," 584.

13. William H. McGuffey, *The Eclectic Second Reader* [. . .] (Cincinnati, 1836), 30–31.

14. William H. McGuffey, *McGuffey's New Third Eclectic Reader: For Young Learners* (Cincinnati, 1865), 94.

15. McGuffey, *The Eclectic Second Reader*, 45.

16. Johann N. Neem, *Democracy's Schools: The Rise of Public Education in America* (Johns Hopkins University Press, 2017), 41.

17. Neem, *Democracy's Schools*, 45.

18. McGuffey, *The Eclectic Second Reader*, 112–15, 128–36. The story of the cherry tree also appears in McGuffey, *McGuffey's New Third Eclectic Reader*, 233–36.

19. McGuffey, *The Eclectic Second Reader*, 138.

20. See, for example, William H. McGuffey, *Eclectic Fourth Reader*, 6th. ed. (Cincinnati, 1838), xi–xii.

21. McGuffey, *Eclectic Fourth Reader*, xii.

22. Douglass, *Narrative of the Life of Frederick Douglass, an American Slave*, 39.

23. David B. Tyack, *The One Best System: A History of American Urban Education* (Harvard University Press, 1974).

24. Zimmerman, *Whose America?*, 11–28.

25. Zimmerman, *Whose America?*, 18.

26. Zimmerman, *Whose America?*, 12–13.

27. Zimmerman, *Whose America?*, 23.

28. Zimmerman, *Whose America?*, 60.

29. Harold Rugg, *Man and His Changing Society* (Ginn, 1930), 2:iv; and Harold Rugg, *Man and His Changing Society*, vol. 5 (Ginn, 1931). Each of the six volumes of the series opens with a preface devoted to these considerations.

30. Harold Rugg, *Man and His Changing Society* (Ginn, 1930), 3:iii.

31. This is even the title of the first chapter of the first volume. Rugg, *Man and His Changing Society* (Ginn, 1929), 1:3.

32. Rugg, *Man and His Changing Society*, 1:10–11.

33. On Morse, see Rugg, *Man and His Changing Society*, 1:323–25. On Bell, see Rugg, *Man and His Changing Society*, 1:329–32.

34. Harold Rugg, *Man and His Changing Society* (Ginn, 1931), 4:14.

35. Rugg, *Man and His Changing Society*, 4:30–46.

36. Rugg, *Man and His Changing Society*, 4:53.

37. Rugg, *Man and His Changing Society*, 4:67, 76, 80.

38. Rugg, *Man and His Changing Society*, 4:85.

39. Rugg, *Man and His Changing Society*, 4:131.

40. Rugg, *Man and His Changing Society*, 4:141.

41. Rugg, *Man and His Changing Society*, 4:146.

42. Rugg, *Man and His Changing Society*, 4:146.

43. Zimmerman, *Whose America?*, 60–61.

44. Adam Laats, *The Other School Reformers: Conservative Activism in American Education* (Harvard University Press, 2015), 75; and Kliebard, *The Struggle for the American Curriculum, 1893–1958*, 172–73.

45. Thomas Bailey, *American Pageant: A History of the Republic*, 5th ed. (D. C. Heath, 1975), 107.

46. I borrow this phrase from the title of one of the most popular textbooks of the past 30 years, Alan Brinkley's *The Unfinished Nation: A Concise History of the American People*.

47. Rugg, *Man and His Changing Society*, 4:14.

48. See, for example, David Randall et al., *Skewed History: Textbook Coverage of Early America and the New Deal*, National Association of Scholars, 2021, https://files.eric.ed.gov/fulltext/ED616081.pdf.

49. Nikole Hannah-Jones et al., eds., *The 1619 Project: A New Origin Story* (One World, 2021), 10–32, 52. Although *The New York Times* describes the book as intended for ninth- through 12th-grade students, the Pulitzer Center's curriculum guides introduce it in middle school, so I will treat it here as an analogue to Rugg's and McGuffey's texts. See, for example, 1619 Project, Education Materials Collection, "What Is the Legacy of Durham's Black Wall Street?," November 2, 2024, https://1619education.org/builder/lesson/what-legacy-durhams-black-wall-street.

50. Hannah-Jones et al., eds., *The 1619 Project*, 452.

51. Hannah-Jones et al., eds., *The 1619 Project*, 452.

52. Sarah Schwartz, "A Wave of New Legislation Aims to Ban DEI in Public Schools," *Education Week*, March 26, 2025, https://www.edweek.org/leadership/a-wave-of-new-legislation-aims-to-ban-dei-in-public-schools/2025/03.

53. Rugg, *Man and His Changing Society*, 4:x.

54. See, for example, Yuval Levin, *A Time to Build: From Family and Community to Congress and the Campus, How Recommitting to Our Institutions Can Revive the American Dream* (Basic Books, 2020), chap. 2.

55. National Assessment of Educational Progress eighth-grade history scores have decreased on average from their peak, in 2010–14, to levels first observed in the initial 1994 test. The share of total American bachelor's degrees in history has fallen from 2.2 percent in 1990 to 1.1 percent in 2021 and in political science from 3.3 percent to 1.9 percent. Nation's Report Card, "NAEP Report Card: U.S. History," https://www.nationsreportcard.gov/ushistory/results/achievement/; US Department of Education, Institute of Education Sciences, National Center for Education Statistics, "Table 325.92. Degrees in Economics, History, Political Science and Government, and Sociology Conferred by Postsecondary Institutions, by Level of Degree: Selected Academic Years, 1949–50 Through 2020–21," 2022, https://nces.ed.gov/programs/digest/d22/tables/dt22_325.92.asp; and US Department of Education, Institute of Education Sciences, National Center for Education Statistics, "Table 318.10. Degrees Conferred by Postsecondary Institutions, by Level of Degree and Sex of Student: Selected Academic Years, 1869–70 Through 2031–32," 2022, https://nces.ed.gov/programs/digest/d22/tables/dt22_318.10.asp.

5

How to Think About America's 250th Birthday

WILFRED MCCLAY

The 250th anniversary of the American founding invites us to consider how to incorporate knowledge about the American Revolution into the education of Americans, in particular the civic education of young Americans. Whether that process might itself be revolutionary, whether it might involve entertaining a new way of thinking about what to do in the field of education, is inevitably part of this question.

One beginning assumption shared by many if not most Americans is that in some way the Revolution and the Declaration of Independence have always been fundamental to our understanding of what America is or what America aspires to be. That assertion may seem so obvious as to be incontestable. But it can present us with a problem if there is not a fairly universal consensus as to what the Revolution was and what it meant, both in its own time and in ours. And if you ask my fellow historians, they will agree on only one thing: that there is no universal consensus. In fact, historians have had lively and consequential debates on these matters for at least the past century.

It would require a bibliographical essay of considerable length to chart all the perspectives that have been on offer, but much of it boils down to the famous dichotomy expressed by the historian Carl Lotus Becker in 1909 between the Revolution understood as a dispute over home rule and the Revolution as a dispute over who would rule at home.[1] Or, more generally, it has been a dispute between interpreting the Revolution as a primarily elite political affair, in which formal political ideas played a central role, or as a burgeoning social revolution, at times bordering on civil war, which (it was hoped) would lead the new country in the direction of a more democratic and egalitarian society—or perhaps fail to do so, thereby leaving the Revolution's potential unfulfilled.

This debate is well worth having, along with its many variants and ancillaries, because it brings out the multifaceted aspects of the American Revolution. We will continue to seek out the Revolution's meanings and debate them precisely because the Revolution is and remains so powerfully central to us as a signal event in which our identity as a people is planted but whose abundant meaning overflows any single attempt to capture and confine it.

That is not how everyone sees the matter, though. In fact, the historian Michael D. Hattem, in an interesting recent book called *The Memory of '76*, has argued that our reliance on the Revolution as a source of national identity and self-definition—he calls the Revolution our "origin myth"—has caused us more trouble than it has been worth. As he puts it, while "the popular memory of the Revolution has been an important vehicle through which Americans have defined and voiced their understanding of the present and their hopes for the future," our origin myth "has been consistently contested" and has shaped conflicts "over partisanship, regionalism, race, gender, class, ethnicity, and religion." He concludes that "remembering the nation's founding has often done far more to divide Americans than it has to unite them" and that "revising the past is an important and long-standing American political tradition."[2]

Taken together, those last two statements would appear to be a bad omen for the forthcoming semiquincentennial of America's birth. Are we to ignore our past or reinvent it? Is that really the choice before us?

Well, this is not the time or place for a book review. But at the risk of failing to do justice to Hattem's book, I would point out two things. First, he does not propose an adequate alternative to our "contested national origin myth."[3] If one is going to introduce anthropological reasoning about these things, one ought to be consistent about it and not use anthropology exclusively as a tool of debunking. If societies need origin myths, then that is a need that cannot be ignored.

Second, it is just possible that a pattern of contestation is not a bug but rather a feature of a free society. It is possible to revere Thomas Jefferson, as many do, yet celebrate living in a society in which Jefferson can be openly derided and even despised as a hypocrite, spendthrift, dilettante, domestic tyrant, racist, and what have you, as many do. Perhaps having a "contested national origin myth" is not such a bad thing if you are interested in having a free society.

What is more, a pattern of contestation is arguably present in all great modern revolutions that have had a lasting impact. On the 200th anniversary of the French Revolution, in 1989, we found out just how ambivalent the French are about the meaning of their own revolution, the iconic modern revolution. Yes, the French nearly all embrace republicanism, which they love so much that just one republic has proven to be not enough for them; there have been five so far, and we are still counting. This is yet another reason why Zhou Enlai's famous statement popularly misunderstood to be in response to a question about the success of the French Revolution—that "it's too early to say"—has lasted so long. Even as apocryphon, the statement carries a certain resonance, a certain plausibility.

But I don't think it would be justifiable to say it's too soon to tell whether the American Revolution has been successful. There is something unique about the role the Revolution has played in American culture as both an agent of stability and an energizing reference point. This paradoxical quality of "the spirit of '76" is made evident by the fact that one of the most conservative organizations in the United States is called the Daughters of the American Revolution. It is also evident in the formulation, favored by liberals, that we have an "unfinished" Revolution. The point is that Americans have looked on the essential character of the Revolution as something to be conserved, protected, revered, and continued. Even amid our modern polarization, we can and should look upon it the same way today.

History as Soulcraft

The propensity to venerate a revolution is not unique to Americans. In 1809, William Wordsworth famously wrote about the French Revolution as it had appeared to its enthusiastic contemporaries:

> Bliss was it in that dawn to be alive,
> But to be young was very heaven!—Oh! times,
> In which the meagre, stale, forbidding ways
> Of custom, law, and statute, took at once
> The attraction of a country in romance![4]

But, of course, that ecstatic, romantic dawn did not last, not for France, and not for Wordsworth.

For most of the 20th century the dominant political party in Mexico was known as the Party of the Institutionalized Revolution (the Partido Revolucionario Institucional). Yet for most of its history that party was as ossified and unrevolutionary as the meticulously preserved corpse of Vladimir Lenin, which has been on display in Moscow's Red Square for over a century. This is perhaps what an institutionalized revolution is destined to look like.

The problem, then, is this: How do we keep the energy of revolution bottled up and yet vital? How do we avoid that descent from aspirational charisma into corpse-cold routinization, the fate Max Weber saw as the eventual fate of all energetic political activity?

Abraham Lincoln worried over a similar problem in his youthful 1838 speech to the Young Men's Lyceum of Springfield, Illinois, which he titled "The Perpetuation of Our Political Institutions." He lamented how the American Revolution's energetic spirit was being overtaken and negated by the growth of lawlessness and violence. The Revolution didn't need to be fought all over again; instead, it needed to be recalled and preserved. Lincoln traced the need for a form of civic education—what he called a "political religion"—centered on inculcating "reverence for the laws" and devotion to reason as keys to the steady perpetuation of our institutions.[5]

We can take Lincoln's thoughts as a starting point in answering this problem for ourselves. If the "spirit of '76," the spirit of the Declaration of Independence, is to be preserved, perpetuated, and perhaps revived, education will have to play a central role. A civic education, an education for republican citizenship grounded in historical knowledge and historical memory, is essential.

And here I must add a personal note. When I was in the process of writing *Land of Hope*, meant as an alternative to the American history textbooks on offer, I happened to have dinner with a then-new friend, an Orthodox Jew and highly accomplished attorney from a white-shoe law firm in New York, who was interested in talking with me about the book. In the course of a lengthy conversation, so lengthy we closed the restaurant down, he said something that made a deep impression on me. "I believe," he offered, "that if our children are taught that they live under a bad regime, it does damage to their souls."

I have not been able to forget his words. And they made me think of the inattention given by those of us who write and teach American history as a profession to the soul-forming aspects of our work. I have sometimes asked colleagues who write in highly critical ways about the American past whether they have any concerns along these lines. The answer I hear is almost always the same: "That's not my job." Just as the surgeon does not have a responsibility to discern the worthiness of the one whose life he saves—and one can be thankful for such professional ethics—so the historian should be guided by the search for truth and nothing else, letting the chips fall where they may, cultivating a critical disposition toward all claims made by and for the past.

But that is an inadequate and, I fear, self-serving comparison. A republican form of government cannot exist for long if it does not elicit the loyalty and love of its citizenry. An education that refuses to address these needs and serve them on a firm and truthful basis will undermine a republic rather than support it. Doing those things is somebody's job. Perhaps America's 250th is the right time to begin thinking about that fact.

The Work of Memory

Looking forward as a nation necessarily means looking backward and remembering. Edmund Burke was getting at this when he famously remarked that "people will not look forward to posterity, who never look backward to their ancestors."[6] Our celebrations in 2026 must involve looking back to the first Fourth of July in 1776, the date on which the United States' status as a free and independent nation was proclaimed to the world. The Declaration of Independence stands at the center of our emergence as a distinct and distinctive people. It produced the enduring flame of the American Revolution, firing the imaginations of the brave men and women who fought to make this country possible against tremendous odds and who saw to it that it would become a beacon to the world.

The study of history has many uses, but primary among them is the work of memory. No great or enduring human enterprise can be sustained without it. No matter how determined and focused we are, we are sure to lose our way unless we regularly look back and reorient ourselves, remembering where and how and why we began, remembering our connection to what came before us, particularly to those people who came before us. Without those points of reference, we not only forget the succession of historical events and the names, places, and stories that form the warp and woof of our common life. We eventually forget who we are.

Let me offer an example to explain what I mean by that rather dramatic statement. The example is drawn not from American history but from a practice begun in the ancient Near East and continuing to this day.

The Passover seder is a ritual meal at the heart of Judaism that involves an annual retelling of the story of the Israelites' miraculous liberation from slavery in ancient Egypt, taken from the book of Exodus in the Bible. The seder itself is based on the biblical verse commanding Jews to retell the story of the Exodus from Egypt: "You shall tell your child on that day, saying, 'It is because of what the Lord did for me when I came out of Egypt.'"[7] It is a story of grateful liberation, a story that defines a people, a story that has helped them remember who they are, year in and year out, through many centuries of tribulation.

The story of the Exodus has been a central part of Western civilization, taking many forms along the way. When it came time for the new United States to design its Great Seal, Benjamin Franklin and Jefferson urged that it should depict the miracle of Exodus and bear the slogan Rebellion to Tyrants Is Obedience to God. Even though it was not adopted, alas, Franklin and Jefferson's design showed an understanding of what Americans most needed to remember about who they are: a free people, under God.[8]

Remembering who we are is not something that comes automatically. And what happens when we are no longer able to manage it? Alzheimer's disease is perhaps the most dreaded affliction of our time. It is dreaded because, by robbing its victims of their memories, it also robs them of their fundamental identity, their very sense of who or what they are. Too many of us today have had the unsettling experience of looking into the eyes of a loved one afflicted with this awful disease and being unsure whether the person we once knew so well is still there behind the eyes, whether he is even capable of remembering who he is or recognizing who we are and the lifelong relationship that has subsisted between us. Without the capacity for memory, such a loved one soon slips away from himself, from us, and from our shared world and finally vanishes into a fog of unknowing.

What is true for individuals is also true for nations and peoples. What memory is for individuals, history is for civilizations. Without the reference points provided by historical memory, we soon forget who we are, and we perish.

Yet there is a crucial difference here. No one can be blamed for having contracted Alzheimer's, an organic condition whose causes we still do not understand. It is not a choice. But we, the American people, can be blamed if we fail to know our own past and fail to pass that knowledge on to the rising generations. We will be the ones responsible for our own decline. And our society has come dangerously close to that state, having lost a general grasp on the larger trajectory of our own history.

The fear that we might lose our national soul by forgetting who we are and where we came from is not something new. The young Lincoln expressed that same anxiety in the Lyceum speech, when he worried that as Americans' memories of the Revolution faded away, so, too, would the underpinnings of the republic itself, the "temple of liberty" that the Revolution had made possible.[9]

In our own time, the problem takes the form of a strange paradox: While we "know" more and more about many details of the American past due to the labors of many battalions of specialized professional historians, we actually *know* less because we lack a grasp of the overarching meaning of our history, the kind of meaning that helps shape the way we live together.

We lack an adequate perspective on our history, a perspective that allows us to see the great achievements of American history in their proper light and properly weighed against that history's admitted failings and shortcomings. We lack a shared sense of how exceptional our pioneering experiment in self-rule has been and how full of darkness and despair and want and iniquity most of human history has been by comparison. A sense of what a brilliant light came into the world with the events of 1776, when for the first time in history a nation explicitly committed itself to the essential equality of all human beings.

An Exceptional Moment

All men may be created equal, as the Declaration of Independence declares, but not all moments are remembered equally. The academic studies of social and cultural historians notwithstanding, our national memory generally does not focus on the vast stretches of ordinary time during which life goes on normally, during which men and women fall in love, have families, raise their children, bury their dead, and carry on with the many small acts of heroism, sacrifice, and devotion that mark the conduct of everyday life—the "unhistoric acts," as George Eliot wrote in the closing words of her great novel *Middlemarch*, of those "who lived faithfully a hidden life, and rest in unvisited tombs."[10]

No, what most people call history is more likely to concern itself with outbursts of the extraordinary, with those events and persons that invade the flow of ordinary time and alter the direction of its currents. The lodestars of popular remembrance emerge during periods and places in which the steady stream of the everyday is interrupted by a concentrated surge of fresh intellectual energy and creative force, and thoughts, discussions, debates, and institutions converge in ways that not only change the way we think but change the world.

These nodes of concentrated activity come to life in groups of people—circles, salons, debating societies, political parties, schools and universities—and not merely in the minds and words of solitary geniuses. Thus we speak in the plural of the founders of the American nation and the framers of the American Constitution. There were singular geniuses in those groups, to be sure. But it's important to stand back and think of the group as a whole, a group that embodies a wider circle of discourse that was capable of sustaining remarkably wise insights into the nature of political society, without which the events and institutions we celebrate as Americans would likely never have come to pass.

Although we often speak of the founders as if they were all of the same mind, it is also important to remember that was definitely not the case. You could drive a truck through the differences between Alexander Hamilton and Jefferson and their wildly divergent visions of the American future. And they were not the only ones to quarrel about the future. A great deal of conflict, debate, jostling, and other forms of vigorous intellectual interchange were an important element in the emergence of the constitutional arrangements that carried the American nation forward into a successful independent existence. Nobody got exactly what he wanted. Yet that state of contention, far from being regrettable, has ultimately been all to our good, since it modeled the kind of political order the Constitution would seek to establish, one built on the recognition of conflict as an inevitable part of all human affairs.

But what kind of conflict? That is an interesting question. To begin answering it, let's consider the titles of three highly interesting and well-regarded recent books on the founding period: *Founding Brothers: The Revolutionary Generation*, by Joseph J. Ellis, winner of the 2000 Pulitzer Prize; *Founding Partisans: Hamilton, Madison, Jefferson, Adams, and the Brawling Birth of American Politics*, by H. W. Brands; and *Friends Divided: John Adams and Thomas Jefferson*, by Gordon S. Wood, arguably the dean of living historians of the United States.

Do you notice the unifying theme here? These founding brothers, they were also quarreling brothers, even brawling brothers. If they were friends, they also were friends often divided. And the political was often the personal. Ellis even argues in his book that the constitutional system of checks and balances was not only a political theory but a practical measure grounded in the experience of disputatious leaders and regions with quite different visions and values. In this view, the Constitution served partly to codify in law the way these quarreling brothers dealt with their disputes.

So what held it all together and made it possible for the nation to run the gauntlet of challenges to the emergence of a free and independent America? What did these figures all have in common? The ground they shared was their awareness of what a great task history had set before them. They knew that a distinct American people now existed, that it was up to them to devise a political regime suitable to govern such a people, and that their actions would to a large extent determine what kind of future lay ahead for this great experiment.

That understanding was a source of energy but also responsibility. And it was a source of joy. Writing on July 3, 1776, John Adams predicted to his wife, Abigail, that the day of independence

> will be the most memorable Epocha, in the History of America.—I am apt to believe that it will be celebrated, by succeeding Generations, as the great anniversary Festival. It ought to be commemorated, as the Day of Deliverance by

> solemn Acts of Devotion to God Almighty. It ought to be solemnized with Pomp and Parade, with Shews, Games, Sports, Guns, Bells, Bonfires and Illuminations from one End of this Continent to the other from this Time forward forever more.[11]

Adams erred only in expecting that July 2 would be the appointed day. He continued,

> You will think me transported with Enthusiasm but I am not.—I am well aware of the Toil and Blood and Treasure, that it will cost Us to maintain this Declaration, and support and defend these States.—Yet through all the Gloom I can see the Rays of ravishing Light and Glory. I can see that the End is more than worth all the Means.[12]

After a war had been fought and a new Constitution drafted, Hamilton amplified the theme, arguing in the heat of the debates over ratification of the new Constitution in 1787 that

> it seems to have been reserved to the people of this country . . . to decide the important question, whether societies of men are really capable . . . of establishing good government from reflection and choice, or whether they are forever destined to depend for their political constitutions on accident and force.[13]

He concluded,

> If there be any truth in the remark, the crisis at which we are arrived may with propriety be regarded as the era in which that decision is to be made; and a wrong election of the part we shall act may, in this view, deserve to be considered as the general misfortune of mankind.[14]

A few years later, George Washington, the greatest hero of the Revolution and the one man to whom all quarreling factions were willing to bow their heads, took the oath of office as president of the national government on a second-floor balcony of Federal Hall in New York City, where an assembled crowd could witness the historic event. Speaking minutes later before a joint session of the new Congress, he declared that "the preservation of the sacred fire of liberty, and the destiny of the Republican model of Government, are . . . staked, on the experiment entrusted to the hands of the American people."[15]

The founders knew they were creating something new, something of the utmost importance, as leaders of citizens, not subjects. They were committed to the creation of a regime that protected the rights and liberties of these self-governing citizens. They also understood the fragility of such arrangements—of all republics throughout recorded history—and understood that anything meriting the label of "experiment" was bound to be a perilous thing, a voyage into uncharted waters, as likely to fail as to succeed.

A Great River of Oratory

Here, then, is another way to think about the 250th anniversary. Let us go back to the beginnings of this foundational voyage, with the document we celebrate every July Fourth—the Declaration of Independence—and its chief author, Thomas Jefferson.

And here a bit of a surprise awaits us. Jefferson's intellectual brilliance was widely known, and he was not a particularly modest man. After all, how many of us design our own tombstones and write our own inscriptions? But in a famous 1825 letter to Henry Lee, he insisted on taking a modest approach to his role as the principal author of the document that has come to stand for the heart and soul of the American Revolution.

It is the best account we have of Jefferson's considered view of the matter, offered in his old age, in the year before his death. The object of the Declaration, he said, was "not to find out new principles, or new arguments, never before thought of, not merely to say things which had never been said before; but to place before mankind the common sense of the subject." It was "neither aiming at originality of principle or sentiment, nor yet copied from any particular and previous writing." Instead, the Declaration "was intended to be an expression of the American mind, and to give to that expression the proper tone and spirit called for by the occasion."[16]

Jefferson's account tells us something important about the diffuse and mingled elements coursing through the words of this great document—and the nation it helped create. There were a great many voices in the air at the time of its creation. To understand the Declaration better, and to understand the various sources of its strength and enduring appeal, we will benefit from a little disentangling so we can better discern some of the distinct voices.

First of all, we should acknowledge that Jefferson was a man of the Enlightenment, and the Declaration is in many ways a document of the Enlightenment, with its emphasis on reason, the natural rights of all human beings, and the consent of the governed as the basis for a free and legitimate government. Think, too, of the Declaration's service as an important inspiration to the French Revolution 13 years later and to similar sociopolitical movements elsewhere, even unto the present day.

So it was an Enlightenment document, but it was not *only* an Enlightenment document. There were many pre-Enlightenment elements in it, background assumptions that have to be taken into account if it is to be fully understood and its authority credited. For example, it drew on the cultural muscle memory of a century and a half of colonial American self-government, which in turn drew on a long tradition of English legal and constitutional practices. This element is what figures most prominently in the list of grievances that forms the bulk of the Declaration. Nearly all of them had to do with the deprivation of *customary* self-rule and the violation of *inherited* rights that were due to the colonists as Englishmen. To put it bluntly, they were used to ruling themselves, as they had done for 150 years or more.

Such appeals differ fundamentally from an appeal to the idea of unalienable natural rights—that is, rights we have merely by virtue of being human—because these former sets of rights are established by precedent, by custom, and are claimed as an inheritance from forebears. In the Declaration's long list of grievances against the British rulers, the king is accused of weakening and dissolving representative bodies, inhibiting the exercise of judiciary powers, imposing unelected and unaccountable imperial officials, quartering standing armies, rendering troops unaccountable to law, and so on.

Such language didn't invoke natural rights but instead referred to specific inherited rights, traceable back through the early modern legal thought of Edward Coke and John Fortescue to the Magna Carta itself, even further back to a shadowy Anglo-Saxon constitution, and then forward through the political struggles of the 17th century, all the way to the Glorious Revolution of 1688, which finally established Parliament's supremacy over the monarchy. Needless to say, the distinction between the two understandings of rights is clearer in definition than in actual practice. Jefferson himself believed the Anglo-Saxon constitution was the "rightful root" of the English constitution even as he believed Americans could appeal to their *natural* rights in declaring independence.[17]

But the larger point here is that an idea of the ancient constitution, and of a historical and traditional transmission and elaboration of its liberties through many centuries of British history, is a part of the story. It forms a vivid and powerful reference point in the background of 18th-century Anglo-American thought. To repeat, the colonists were used to ruling themselves, because they thought of themselves as Englishmen with the customary inherited rights of Englishmen. The Declaration appealed to that sentiment.

Finally, we should stress the immense influence of the colonists' religious sentiments as a background element in American revolutionary sentiment. To be sure, Jefferson does not mention this in his letter to Lee, in keeping with his well-established reputation as a skeptic and critic of religious orthodoxy. But it is highly significant that, as noted above,

Jefferson and Franklin both urged that the Great Seal of the United States should depict the Exodus, the Bible's great foundational story of the Jewish people, in which the Israelites escaped their captivity as slaves in Egypt with a dramatic parting of the waters of the Red Sea and came into freedom in the land God had promised them. Franklin described his idea for the seal's design in this way:

> Moses standing on the Shore, and extending his Hand over the Sea, thereby causing the same to overwhelm Pharoah who is sitting in an open Chariot, a Crown on his Head and a Sword in his hand. Rays from a Pillar of Fire in the Clouds reaching to Moses, to express that he acts by Command of the Deity.
>
> Motto, *Rebellion to Tyrants Is Obedience to God.*[18]

Nor was this profoundly religious symbolism offered as a form of pandering, throwing a bit of religion into the mix for the uneducated rubes. Jefferson liked the motto so much he used it on his own personal seal.[19]

The story of the Exodus is not merely a story for the Jewish people. You see it wherever you look in American history. The New England Puritans viewed their perilous ocean crossing in search of religious liberty as a repetition of the Israelites' flight to freedom, bringing them into Zion. The Latter-day Saints who made the trek to the Salt Lake Valley under the leadership of Brigham Young, seeking relief from the relentless persecution to which they had been subjected, saw themselves in a similar light. Enslaved Africans and African Americans south of the Ohio River also looked to the Exodus story as an anticipatory symbol of their own eventual freedom as they sang, "Go down, Moses. . . . Tell old Pharaoh / Let my people go." Jefferson saw the Exodus as an image of the Enlightenment, "the signal of arousing men to burst the chains, under which Monkish ignorance and superstition had persuaded them to bind themselves, and to assume the blessings & security of self government."[20]

And for all of Jefferson's reputation as a religious skeptic, he penned no more searing words than these in his 1785 book, *Notes on the State of*

Virginia, which are inscribed on the northeast portico of the Jefferson Memorial in Washington, DC:

> Can the liberties of a nation be thought secure when we have removed their only firm basis, a conviction in the minds of the people that these liberties are the gift of God? That they are not to be violated but with his wrath? Indeed I tremble for my country when I reflect that God is just: that his justice cannot sleep for ever.[21]

But religion's influence on the revolutionary cause went much, much deeper than the ideas of elite leaders such as Jefferson and Franklin. Eighteenth-century British North American religious life was dominated by Reformed Protestantism, expressed vividly in revolutionary-era sermons, public documents, newspaper editorials, and political pamphlets. In such communities, there was a pervasive belief in the doctrine of original sin, which led to a deep suspicion of any form of concentrated power and opposition to imperial intrusions on American life—particularly when coming from a mother country whose culture was seen as arrogant and corrupt.

Britain's corruption became fodder for countless sermons. These powerful, evangelistic sermons were a major contributor to not only the rising sense of American national self-consciousness but especially the rising revolutionary sentiment of the 1770s, when it is estimated that as many as 80 percent of political pamphlets were reprinted sermons.[22] Clearly the connection between religious sentiments and political activity was strong.

Adams was no stranger to questions of political theory, and his 1776 *Thoughts on Government* became a guide to the drafting of state constitutions. But Adams understood that a growing undercurrent of popular disaffection was a far more potent cause of the Revolution than any particular philosophical question. As he wrote in his own retrospective of the struggle for independence in 1818:

> The Revolution was effected before the War commenced. The Revolution was in the Minds and Hearts of the People. A Change in their Religious Sentiments of their Duties and Obligations. While the King, and all in Authority under him, were believed to govern, in Justice and Mercy according to the Laws and Constitutions derived to them from the God of Nature, and transmitted to them by their Ancestors—they thought themselves bound to pray for the King and Queen and all the Royal Family, and all the Authority under them, as Ministers ordained of God for their good. But when they Saw those Powers renouncing all the Principles of Authority, and bent up on the destruction of all the Securities of their Lives, Liberties and Properties, they thought it their Duty to pray for the Continental Congress and all the thirteen State Congresses, &c.[23]

In other words, rebellion to tyrants was obedience to God.

So the Declaration should be understood as a great river of oratory that was fed by different streams, a document that held together a variety of perspectives thanks to the literary skill of its principal author, Jefferson, and by the needs of the moment in which it appeared. Its enduring appeal, as it approaches its 250th anniversary, is nothing short of remarkable.

Anniversaries Past and Present

This brings us to a final way of thinking about our great national anniversary, and that is to reflect on the ways we have thought about it in the past. It has not always been the same.

The 50th anniversary of the American Revolution was an astonishing moment because it was marked by the near-simultaneous deaths of Jefferson and Adams. The fact that two of the nation's most distinguished founders, the second and third presidents, died on July 4, 1826, exactly five decades after the Continental Congress adopted the Declaration of

Independence, was widely seen as a symbolic end to the revolutionary generation, prompting both pride and apprehension about the future prospects for the nation's founding principles. Was God telling America something about the fate of its Revolution? If so, what? Approving or disapproving? Either was possible.

Twenty-six years later, Frederick Douglass's 1852 speech "What to the Slave Is the Fourth of July?" combined high praise for the founders, the Declaration, and the Constitution with scalding criticism of the country's failure to live up to these revolutionary principles.[24] It was a profound commentary on the gap between our ideals and our actions and a harbinger of the civil war that was coming. But it was also a strong endorsement of the document to which the nation would have to return to reorder itself and find its way anew.

The nation's 100th anniversary, in 1876, the first major observance since the end of the Civil War, was marked by a proclamation from President Ulysses S. Grant suffused with religious overtones, emphasizing thanksgiving to God and prayers for His continued favor.[25]

And then there was President Calvin Coolidge's speech commemorating the 150th anniversary of the Revolution, in July 1926.[26] It was a defense of America's founding principles against progressives like Woodrow Wilson, who believed the massive social and economic changes in American life in the early 20th century had invalidated those principles and required modern theories of government to take their place. It was a speech that stands in the line of great presidential rhetoric from Washington to Jefferson, to Lincoln, to Franklin Delano Roosevelt, to Ronald Reagan. Coolidge reminded Americans then and now of the exceptional character of their own revolution and the enduring importance of liberty and equality as natural rights:

> About the Declaration there is a finality that is exceedingly restful. It is often asserted that the world has made a great deal of progress since 1776, that we have had new thoughts and new experiences which have given us a great advance over the

> people of that day, and that we may therefore very well discard their conclusions for something more modern. But that reasoning can not be applied to this great charter. If all men are created equal, that is final. If they are endowed with inalienable rights, that is final. If governments derive their just powers from the consent of the governed, that is final. No advance, no progress can be made beyond these propositions. If anyone wishes to deny their truth or their soundness, the only direction in which he can proceed historically is not forward, but backward toward the time when there was no equality, no rights of the individual, no rule of the people. Those who wish to proceed in that direction can not lay claim to progress. They are reactionary. Their ideas are not more modern, but more ancient, than those of the Revolutionary fathers.[27]

These are words that Americans today, almost a century later, living in the second quarter of the 21st century, may be ready to hear afresh. Perhaps the way forward begins by looking backward.

Many of us feel obliged to look back at 1776 in as critical and dry-eyed a manner as possible, in a manner that not only takes full and honest account of the founders' moral and intellectual failings but places those failings before all else when reflecting on our past. I think there is much about this disposition that speaks well of us. We are not afraid to be self-critical and to carry out our self-criticism in public, in the full view of the world. Our chief rivals, and even some of our allies, believe otherwise. They believe this openness weakens them. We believe the opposite is true.

But self-criticism can easily go too far and lead us into cynicism. Its excesses are as dangerous as those of self-congratulation. A mature perspective on our past demands more of us than that. It demands that we seek a balance, with a full awareness of the fact that in the real world, ideals are often ignored and heroes are always going to be flawed. Yet we do ourselves and the rising generations of our young people no favors if we deny the greatness of what our country has achieved and its potential to achieve much more in the years ahead. We should affirm that greatness, not least for the sake of those who are coming of age today and looking for fields of endeavor that will prove fulfilling and admirable.

The Formation of Republican Souls

And here I come to that "not our job" aspect of education that we ignore at our peril. Of course, history must be based on truth, not on pleasing or manipulative fictions. We do ourselves and our young no favors by prettifying or oversimplifying the past and failing to give an honest account of our failures as well as our triumphs.

But we also do no favors to ourselves or the truth if we fail to honor the magnificent achievements of our history and leave them out of our accounting, as has become too often the case. We need to remember that one of the civic functions of history, one of the chief reasons we endeavor to record the past and teach it to our young, is to serve as a vessel of shared memory, imparting to each generation a sense of membership in its own society, a sense of living connection to its own past—a sense that can unite us and sustain us in hard times.

Lincoln brought that sense of historical connection to many of his best speeches, most notably to his great speech at the dedication of the Soldiers' National Cemetery in Gettysburg on November 19, 1863. Even as the war raged around him, he reached back to the nation's birth in 1776 as one of the great achievements in human history, a precious legacy to whose preservation the deeds of the present ought to be dedicated.[28] He found in the American past a source of sustenance, a steadying influence in a time buffeted by chaos and fear, a source of renewed courage and determination.

And so can it be for us. Our young people deserve nothing less. We are failing them and our country so long as we fail to give them a rich and sustaining sense of their own past, a sense that is both truthful and inspiring. It's high time we did. For consider the alternative: If a great story of estimable things can give us courage and hope in a hard time, does it not stand to reason that the promulgation of a dishonorable story of relentless failure, mendacity, and despoliation can have the opposite effect?

For the inglorious story, too, is a kind of civic education. We are tenderly solicitous of the "safety" of college students who may be exposed to ideas or words they may find upsetting. But why do we not think about the effects of the inglorious story they are taking in? Doesn't their picture of the world they inhabit profoundly affect their sense of their life's possibilities and prospects? Shouldn't we consider whether the remarkably high indicators of unhappiness among our young people—and not only young people—are traceable partly to a massive loss of morale and hope?[29]

I'm concerned about these statistics, as any sensible person should be. It is hard not to think they presage a kind of general moral collapse in our society. No one would deny there are material factors behind them, such as the dizzying changes in the structures of the national and world economy. But a nation's morale is ultimately a question of spirit more than matter.

One cannot deny that by moving into the vacuum left by the absence of a genuine civic education, the decline of religion, and the decay of traditional structures of family life, the inglorious story has been gaining the upper hand on us, playing a powerful role in sustaining our low morale; saturating our young in debilitating ideas about the past, present, and future; and leaving them isolated and anxious. Many of my students tell me, without irony, that they believe the present day is the worst time in all human history. Imagine what will become of them when we experience really tough times, as we are sure to do, and perhaps sooner than we think.

As the great Austrian psychiatrist Victor Frankl observed, we humans can bear almost any kind of material deprivation and suffering—except the deprivation of meaning. "He who has a *why* to live for," Frankl wrote, "can bear with almost any *how*."[30] And without that *why*, almost any *how* can defeat us and overturn our best intentions and hopes. Such matters go far deeper than civics. But it is not too much to claim that a robust civic education, which seeks to impart a sense of continuity with generations gone before and begins the process of locating one's life in a meaning far larger than oneself, is an important step back from the lonely precipice on whose brink we find ourselves. We don't have a moment to lose in getting started.

What about the all-too-human leaders who brought our nation into being? We can teach our children this: Flawed people are normal. But what is not normal or usual are those rare moments in history when flawed people come together to produce great things. Not flawless things, but great things, worthy of our admiration and gratitude. The collection of remarkable men and women present at our beginning, at that remarkable juncture of human history 250 years ago—each of them contributed something to the outcome. Even as they quarreled.

We've never stopped quarreling. You may have noticed that we are still quarreling today. And yet we have held together. Perhaps for the 250th, we should give thanks for that fact and at least take time out from our quarrels long enough to lift a toast to those who helped make our tradition of quarreling possible. And to one another, whose job it is to carry on.

Notes

1. Carl Lotus Becker, *The History of Political Parties in the Province of New York, 1760–1776* (University of Wisconsin, 1909), 22.

2. Michael D. Hattem, *The Memory of '76: The Revolution in American History* (Yale University Press, 2025), 303–4.

3. Hattem, *The Memory of '76*, 1.

4. William Wordsworth, "The French Revolution as It Appeared to Enthusiasts at Its Commencement," Poetry Foundation, 1809, https://www.poetryfoundation.org/poems/45518/the-french-revolution-as-it-appeared-to-enthusiasts-at-its-commencement.

5. Abraham Lincoln, "The Perpetuation of Our Political Institutions," speech, Young Men's Lyceum of Springfield, IL, January 27, 1838, https://www.abrahamlincolnonline.org/lincoln/speeches/lyceum.htm.

6. Edmund Burke, *Reflections on the Revolution in France*, ed. J. G. A. Pocock (1790; Hackett, 1987), 48.

7. Exod. 13:8.

8. Anna Berkes, "Personal Seal," Monticello, October 4, 2007, https://www.monticello.org/research-education/thomas-jefferson-encyclopedia/personal-seal/.

9. Lincoln, "The Perpetuation of Our Political Institutions."

10. George Eliot, *Middlemarch* (1871–72; Wordsworth Classics, 1987), 688.

11. John Adams to Abigail Adams, July 3, 1776, Massachusetts Historical Society, Adams Family Papers, https://www.masshist.org/digitaladams/archive/doc?id=L17760703jasecond.

12. Adams to Adams, July 3, 1776.

13. *Federalist*, no. 1 (Alexander Hamilton), https://guides.loc.gov/federalist-papers/text-1-10.

14. *Federalist*, no. 1 (Hamilton).

15. George Washington, "First Inaugural Address," speech, Federal Hall, New York, Founders Online, https://founders.archives.gov/documents/Washington/05-02-02-0130-0003.

16. Thomas Jefferson to Henry Lee, May 8, 1825, Founders Online, https://founders.archives.gov/documents/Jefferson/98-01-02-5212.

17. Thomas Jefferson to John Cartwright, June 5, 1824, Founders Online, https://founders.archives.gov/documents/Jefferson/98-01-02-4313.

18. Benjamin Franklin, "Proposal for the Great Seal of the United States," before August 14, 1776, Founders Online, https://founders.archives.gov/documents/Franklin/01-22-02-0330.

19. Berkes, "Personal Seal."

20. Thomas Jefferson to Roger Chew Weightman, June 24, 1826, https://founders.archives.gov/documents/Jefferson/98-01-02-6179.

21. Monticello, "Quotations on the Jefferson Memorial," https://www.monticello.org/research-education/thomas-jefferson-encyclopedia/quotations-jefferson-memorial/; and National Park Service, "Northeast Portico: Thomas Jefferson Memorial," https://www.nps.gov/places/northeast-chamber-panel.htm.

22. Glenn A. Moots, "Early America's Political Pulpit," *Law & Liberty*, December 28, 2021, https://lawliberty.org/classic/early-americas-political-pulpit/.

23. John Adams to Hezekiah Niles, February 13, 1818, Founders Online, https://founders.archives.gov/documents/Adams/99-02-02-6854.

24. Frederick Douglass, "What to the Slave Is the Fourth of July?," National Constitution Center, 1852, https://constitutioncenter.org/the-constitution/historic-document-library/detail/frederick-douglass-what-to-the-slave-is-the-fourth-of-july-1852.

25. Ulysses S. Grant, "Proclamation Celebrating the Hundredth Anniversary of Independence," University of Virginia, Miller Center, June 26, 1876, https://millercenter.org/the-presidency/presidential-speeches/june-26-1876-proclamation-celebrating-hundredth-anniversary.

26. Calvin Coolidge, "Address at the Celebration of the 150th Anniversary of the Declaration of Independence in Philadelphia, Pennsylvania," speech, Philadelphia,

July 5, 1924, https://www.presidency.ucsb.edu/documents/address-the-celebration-the-150th-anniversary-the-declaration-independence-philadelphia.

27. Coolidge, "Address at the Celebration of the 150th Anniversary of the Declaration of Independence in Philadelphia, Pennsylvania."

28. Abraham Lincoln, "The Gettysburg Address," speech, Gettysburg, PA, November 19, 1863, https://www.abrahamlincolnonline.org/lincoln/speeches/gettysburg.htm.

29. Harvard Kennedy School, Institute of Politics, "Harvard Youth Poll," Fall 2025, https://iop.harvard.edu/youth-poll/51st-edition-fall-2025.

30. Victor E. Frankl, *Man's Search for Meaning*, trans. Ilse Lasch (1946; Beacon Press, 2006), 76, 104.

About the Authors

Richard Brookhiser is an American journalist, biographer, and historian. He is a senior editor at *National Review*. He is most widely known for a series of biographies of America's founders, including Alexander Hamilton, Gouverneur Morris, and George Washington.

Allen C. Guelzo is a nonresident senior fellow at the American Enterprise Institute and a professor of humanities at the Hamilton School for Classical and Civic Education at the University of Florida. He is the author of *Abraham Lincoln: Redeemer President* (1999), among many other books.

Jane Kamensky is president and CEO of Monticello and the Thomas Jefferson Foundation. She was the Jonathan Trumbull Professor of American History at Harvard University and is the author of *A Revolution in Color: The World of John Singleton Copley* (2016), among many other books.

Rita Koganzon is an associate professor at the School of Civic Life and Leadership at the University of North Carolina and the author of *Liberal States, Authoritarian Families: Childhood and Education in Early Modern Thought* (2021).

Wilfred McClay is the Victor Davis Hanson Chair in Classical History and Western Civilization at Hillsdale College and the author of *The Masterless: Self and Society in Modern America* (1994).

About the Editors

Yuval Levin is the director of Social, Cultural, and Constitutional Studies at the American Enterprise Institute, where he also holds the Beth and Ravenel Curry Chair in Public Policy. The founder and editor of *National Affairs*, he is also a senior editor at *The New Atlantis*, a contributing editor at *National Review*, and a contributing opinion writer at *The New York Times*.

Adam J. White is the Laurence H. Silberman Chair in Constitutional Governance and a senior fellow at the American Enterprise Institute, where he focuses on the Supreme Court and the administrative state. Concurrently, he directs the Antonin Scalia Law School's C. Boyden Gray Center for the Study of the Administrative State.

John Yoo is a nonresident senior fellow at the American Enterprise Institute; the Emanuel S. Heller Professor of Law at the University of California, Berkeley; and a senior research fellow at the Civitas Institute at the University of Texas at Austin.

The American Enterprise Institute for Public Policy Research

AEI is a nonpartisan, nonprofit research and educational organization. The work of our scholars and staff advances ideas rooted in our commitment to expanding individual liberty, increasing opportunity, and strengthening freedom.

The Institute engages in research; publishes books, papers, studies, and short-form commentary; and conducts seminars and conferences. AEI's research activities are carried out under four major departments: Domestic Policy Studies, Economic Policy Studies, Foreign and Defense Policy Studies, and Social, Cultural, and Constitutional Studies. The resident scholars and fellows listed in these pages are part of a network that also includes nonresident scholars at top universities.

The views expressed in AEI publications are those of the authors; AEI does not take institutional positions on any issues.

RESEARCH STAFF

SAMUEL J. ABRAMS
Nonresident Senior Fellow

BETH AKERS
Senior Fellow

J. JOEL ALICEA
Nonresident Fellow

JOSEPH ANTOS
Senior Fellow Emeritus

LEON ARON
Senior Fellow Emeritus

JOHN BAILEY
Nonresident Senior Fellow

KYLE BALZER
Fellow

CLAUDE BARFIELD
Senior Fellow

MICHAEL BARONE
Senior Fellow Emeritus

MICHAEL BECKLEY
Nonresident Senior Fellow

ERIC J. BELASCO
Nonresident Senior Fellow

ANDREW G. BIGGS
Senior Fellow

MASON M. BISHOP
Nonresident Fellow

DAN BLUMENTHAL
Senior Fellow

KARLYN BOWMAN
Distinguished Senior Fellow Emeritus

HAL BRANDS
Senior Fellow

ALEX BRILL
Senior Fellow

ARTHUR C. BROOKS
President Emeritus

DANIEL BUCK
Research Fellow

RICHARD BURKHAUSER
Nonresident Senior Fellow

CLAY CALVERT
Nonresident Senior Fellow

JAMES C. CAPRETTA
Senior Fellow; Milton Friedman Chair

NICHOLAS CARL
Fellow

TIMOTHY P. CARNEY
Senior Fellow

BRIAN CARTER
Fellow

AMITABH CHANDRA
Nonresident Senior Fellow

LYNNE V. CHENEY
Distinguished Senior Fellow

YVONNE CHIU
Jeane Kirkpatrick Visiting Fellow

JAMES W. COLEMAN
Nonresident Senior Fellow

HEATHER A. CONLEY
Nonresident Senior Fellow

PRESTON COOPER
Senior Fellow

ZACK COOPER
Senior Fellow

KEVIN CORINTH
Senior Fellow; Deputy Director, Center on Opportunity and Social Mobility; Daniel C. Searle Chair

JAY COST
Gerald R. Ford Nonresident Senior Fellow

DANIEL A. COX
Senior Fellow in Polling and Public Opinion; Director, Survey Center on American Life

SADANAND DHUME
Senior Fellow

ROSS DOUTHAT
Nonresident Fellow

LAURA DOVE
Nonresident Fellow

COLIN DUECK
Nonresident Senior Fellow

MACKENZIE EAGLEN
Senior Fellow

NICHOLAS EBERSTADT
Henry Wendt Chair in Political Economy

JEFFREY EISENACH
Nonresident Senior Fellow

CHRISTINE EMBA
Senior Fellow

RYAN FEDASIUK
Fellow

ANDREW FERGUSON
Nonresident Fellow

JESÚS FERNÁNDEZ-VILLAVERDE
Nonresident Senior Fellow

JOHN G. FERRARI
Nonresident Senior Fellow

JOHN C. FORTIER
Senior Fellow

ANEMONE FRANZ
Visiting Research Fellow

AARON FRIEDBERG
Nonresident Senior Fellow

JOSEPH B. FULLER
Nonresident Senior Fellow

ARTHUR GAILES
Research Fellow

SCOTT GANZ
Nonresident Fellow

R. RICHARD GEDDES
Nonresident Senior Fellow

ROBERT P. GEORGE
Nonresident Senior Fellow

EDWARD L. GLAESER
Nonresident Senior Fellow

JOSEPH W. GLAUBER
Nonresident Senior Fellow

JONAH GOLDBERG
Senior Fellow; Asness Chair in Applied Liberty

SAMUEL GOLDMAN
Visiting Fellow

JACK GOLDSMITH
Nonresident Senior Fellow

BARRY K. GOODWIN
Nonresident Senior Fellow

SCOTT GOTTLIEB, MD
Senior Fellow

PHIL GRAMM
Nonresident Senior Fellow

WILLIAM C. GREENWALT
Senior Fellow

ALLEN C. GUELZO
Nonresident Senior Fellow

PHILIP HAMBURGER
Nonresident Senior Fellow

JIM HARPER
Nonresident Senior Fellow

TODD HARRISON
Senior Fellow

WILLIAM HAUN
Nonresident Fellow

FREDERICK M. HESS
Senior Fellow; Director, Education Policy Studies

CAROLE HOOVEN
Nonresident Senior Fellow

BRONWYN HOWELL
Nonresident Senior Fellow

R. GLENN HUBBARD
Nonresident Senior Fellow

HOWARD HUSOCK
Senior Fellow

DAVID HYMAN, MD
John H. Makin Visiting Scholar

BENEDIC N. IPPOLITO
Senior Fellow

MARK JAMISON
Nonresident Senior Fellow

FREDERICK W. KAGAN
Senior Fellow; Director, Critical Threats Project

CHARLES N. KAHN III
Visiting Senior Fellow

STEVEN B. KAMIN
Senior Fellow

LEON R. KASS, MD
Senior Fellow Emeritus

JOSHUA T. KATZ
Senior Fellow

L. LYNNE KIESLING
Nonresident Senior Fellow

KLON KITCHEN
Nonresident Senior Fellow

KEVIN R. KOSAR
Senior Fellow

PAUL H. KUPIEC
Arthur F. Burns Senior Fellow in Financial Policy

DESMOND LACHMAN
Senior Fellow

CHARLES LANE
Nonresident Senior Fellow

PAUL LETTOW
Senior Fellow

DANIEL LYONS
Nonresident Senior Fellow

NAT MALKUS
Senior Fellow; Deputy Director, Education Policy Studies

JOHN D. MAURER
Nonresident Fellow

ELAINE MCCUSKER
Senior Fellow

BRUCE D. MEYER
Nonresident Senior Fellow

CHRIS MILLER
Nonresident Senior Fellow

THOMAS P. MILLER
Senior Fellow

M. ANTHONY MILLS
Senior Fellow; Director, Center for Technology, Science, and Energy

FERDINANDO MONTE
Nonresident Senior Fellow

CHARLES MURRAY
F. A. Hayek Chair Emeritus in Cultural Studies

STEPHEN D. OLINER
Senior Fellow Emeritus

BRENT ORRELL
Senior Fellow

TOBIAS PETER
Senior Fellow; Codirector, AEI Housing Center

JAMES PETHOKOUKIS
Senior Fellow; Editor, AEIdeas Blog; DeWitt Wallace Chair

ROGER PIELKE JR.
Senior Fellow

EDWARD J. PINTO
Senior Fellow; Codirector, AEI Housing Center

DANIELLE PLETKA
Distinguished Senior Fellow

KYLE POMERLEAU
Senior Fellow

ROBERT PONDISCIO
Senior Fellow

RAMESH PONNURU
Nonresident Senior Fellow

ROB PORTMAN
Distinguished Visiting Fellow in the Practice of Public Policy

ANGELA RACHIDI
Senior Fellow; Rowe Scholar

NAOMI SCHAEFER RILEY
Senior Fellow

WILL RINEHART
Senior Fellow

DALIBOR ROHAC
Senior Fellow

CHRISTINE ROSEN
Senior Fellow

JEFFREY A. ROSEN
Nonresident Senior Fellow

MICHAEL M. ROSEN
Nonresident Senior Fellow

IAN ROWE
Senior Fellow

MICHAEL RUBIN
Senior Fellow

PAUL RYAN
Distinguished Visiting Fellow in the Practice of Public Policy

DANIEL J. SAMET
Jeane Kirkpatrick Fellow

BEN SASSE
Nonresident Senior Fellow

SALLY SATEL, MD
Senior Fellow

ERIC SAYERS
Nonresident Fellow

CHRISTOPHER J. SCALIA
Senior Fellow

BRETT D. SCHAEFER
Senior Fellow

DIANA SCHAUB
Nonresident Senior Fellow

ANNA SCHERBINA
Nonresident Senior Fellow

GARY J. SCHMITT
Senior Fellow

MARK SCHNEIDER
Nonresident Senior Fellow

DEREK SCISSORS
Senior Fellow

NEENA SHENAI
Nonresident Fellow

DAN SLATER
Nonresident Fellow

SITA NATARAJ SLAVOV
Nonresident Senior Fellow

THOMAS W. SMITH
Nonresident Fellow

VINCENT H. SMITH
Nonresident Senior Fellow

CHRISTINA HOFF SOMMERS
Senior Fellow Emeritus

ANGELA STENT
Senior Fellow

DANIEL STID
Senior Fellow

CHRIS STIREWALT
Senior Fellow

BENJAMIN STOREY
Senior Fellow; Ravenel Curry Chair in Civic Thought; Codirector, Center for the Future of the American University

JENNA SILBER STOREY
Senior Fellow; Ravenel Curry Chair in Civic Thought; Codirector, Center for the Future of the American University

DANIEL A. SUMNER
Visiting Senior Fellow in Economic Studies

RUY TEIXEIRA
Nonresident Senior Fellow

SHANE TEWS
Nonresident Senior Fellow

MARC A. THIESSEN
Senior Fellow

JOSEPH S. TRACY
Nonresident Senior Fellow

SEAN TRENDE
Nonresident Fellow

TUNKU VARADARAJAN
Nonresident Fellow

STAN VEUGER
Senior Fellow

ALAN D. VIARD
Senior Fellow Emeritus

DUSTIN WALKER
Nonresident Fellow

PHILIP WALLACH
Senior Fellow

PETER J. WALLISON
Senior Fellow Emeritus

MARK J. WARSHAWSKY
Senior Fellow; Wilson H. Taylor Chair in Health Care and Retirement Policy

MATT WEIDINGER
Senior Fellow; Rowe Scholar

ADAM J. WHITE
Senior Fellow; Laurence H. Silberman Chair in Constitutional Governance

BRAD WILCOX
Nonresident Senior Fellow

THOMAS CHATTERTON WILLIAMS
Nonresident Fellow

SCOTT WINSHIP
Senior Fellow; Director, Center on Opportunity and Social Mobility

AUDRYE WONG
Nonresident Senior Fellow

JOHN YOO
Nonresident Senior Fellow

BENJAMIN ZYCHER
Senior Fellow

www.ingramcontent.com/pod-product-compliance
Lightning Source LLC
LaVergne TN
LVHW051006080826
845145LV00009B/2488

9780844751153